Praise for

God is the Cure, Love is the Answer

Nikolov's complex, searching memoir details the severe abuse and trauma which impacted the trajectory of her life. It is also a cathartic account of the faith she steadfastly holds for survival and how her belief in God enables her to transcend the darkness.

This is a profoundly moving and gracefully rendered memoir of a broken woman's triumph against the darkness surrounding her.

— **Dylan Ward**, US Review of Books

***

Nikolov maintains a mastery over a narrative she never loses control of. It is a timely book and one that joins the ranks of well-remembered memoirs. It is a candid story of a woman's fight with the demons that torture her and the victory over them. She skillfully explores within these pages the horror and the goodness of our humanity and how one can persevere in the face of tremendous odds. By its end, the reader will no doubt respect her and feel compelled to share her story.

— US Review

***

Aimee Cabo Nikolov's memoir, *God is the Cure, Love is the Answer*, is a story of true grit, courage and impenetrable faith.

I am in absolute awe of this woman's tenacious style in capturing the essence through words of how she faced her demons and recounts the horrors of a childhood that was unquestionably ripped from her by her parents. Through graphic and succinct prose, she plants her pen solidly from page to page and shares intimate details of wrongs with unfathomable depth. In my opinion, we are a society drawn to memoirs of iconic Hollywood types or war criminals or psychopathic dregs of society. The fame tied to the subject draws the audience in. Rarely do we hear the story of one of, in my opinion, many innocent unknowns who have been robbed of their youth and left with the burden of physical and emotional scars they must carry the remainder of their lives. I thank Ms. Nikolov for her profound writing in telling her horrific truths. I also commend her for her bravery in doing so. She certainly exposed the monsters who surrounded (and continue to surround) her life through the power of her pen. Exceptional writing! Quill says: *God is the Cure, Love is the Answer* is not only an apropos title, but it's also a beacon of light to shine on how to overcome and cope with egregious tragedies bestowed upon a human life.

— *Feathered Quill Book Reviews*

***

God Is The Cure, Love Is The Answer, by Aimee Cabo Nikolov, is the very tragic and at the same time very inspirational story of a woman who not only survived but prevailed against all odds.

I applaud the author for having the strength to share her story so others might find their own strength to go on, and also for utilizing her faith to eventually find love and hope…

—*Carol Hoyer for Reader Views.*

***

I am truly amazed at how well Aimee was able to survive mentally and physically with all she endured. All I can say is "Good for you, Aimee."

The author has written with honesty and passion and, above all else, has given readers hope if they or someone they know is experiencing this type of situation. Her story educates readers about abuse and family neglect and is truly inspirational. Hopefully, it will provide readers with a better insight into those who are in this position and how, most of all, we should not judge.

—*Carol Hoyer for Reader Views.*

***

The story is told honestly, clearly and without frills. Each chapter takes you further on her journey and, just when you think she is safe, she isn't. Ms. Nikolov's honesty and kindness always shine through and the book inspires with how a soul that believes manages to always find the way to the Good. Ms. Nikolov built a life all of us can admire, with having had everything against her.

The book, even with all the sadness of her life, is upbeat and a beautiful romance. It proves that all of us can overcome with an insistence and willingness to go toward Love.

—*Gay Walley*

***

There are certain events that change the course of a life irrevocably. After enduring terrible sexual abuse as a child, Aimee Cabo Nikolov had to overcome homelessness, substance abuse, and years of custody battles to create a better future for her first daughter. In her debut memoir, *God is the Answer, Love is the Cure*, Nikolov tells her story with honesty and vulnerability. What in the beginning reads as a tragedy transforms into a story about falling in love—with the right man and with life itself—showing the reader that no tragedy is too great to overcome and how hope and faith can guide us through even the darkest of times.

—*Angelina Carter, Book Reviewer*

***

I truly admire Aimee's strength and bravery. She has endured unimaginable pain and devastation but maintains a strong sense of faith and optimism. This is a well-written and well-organized book. Aimee's story is a thrilling, yet in many ways romantic, page-turner.

—*Jessica Wheeler, book reviewer*

***

A heartrending memoir that brings to light the terminal effects of child sexual abuse. It captures Aimee Cabo Nikolov's difficult journey to finding her place in a cruel world.

—*Emunah Anne, book reviewer*

God is the Cure, Love is the Answer

A Memoir

Aimee Cabo Nikolov

Published by KHARIS PUBLISHING, imprint of KHARIS MEDIA LLC.

Copyright © 2022 Aimee Cabo Nikolov

ISBN-13: 978-1-63746-194-5

ISBN-10: 1-63746-194-1

Library of Congress Control Number: 2022948878

Scriptures taken from THE HOLY BIBLE, ENGLISH STANDARD VERSION ® Copyright© 2001 by Crossway, a publishing ministry of Good News Publishers. Used by permission.

All KHARIS PUBLISHING products are available at special quantity discounts for bulk purchase for sales promotions, premiums, fund-raising, and educational needs. For details, contact:

Kharis Media LLC

Tel: 1-479-599-8657
support@kharispublishing.com
www.kharispublishing.com

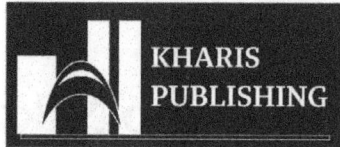
KHARIS PUBLISHING

To my wonderful husband, Bobby, my children, Danielle, Sean, and Michelle, and to all those who have believed they cannot survive their past.
We can do more than that. We can be beacons of light.

Table of Contents

Prologue..*xi*

Chapter 1..13

Chapter 2..20

Chapter 3..24

Chapter 4..29

Chapter 5..34

Chapter 6..38

Chapter 7..42

Chapter 8..48

Chapter 9..52

Chapter 10 55

Chapter 11 60

Chapter 12..65

Chapter 13 68

Chapter 14 72

Chapter 15 77

Chapter 16 82

Chapter 17 86

Chapter 18 96

Chapter 19 103

Chapter 20 109

Chapter 21 115

Chapter 22 118

Chapter 23 124

Chapter 24 130

Chapter 26 142

Chapter 27 148

About Kharis Publishing *152*

Prologue

Chapter 1

Hail Mary, full of grace, the Lord is with you.
Blessed are you among women,
and blessed is the fruit of your womb, Jesus.
Holy Mary, Mother of God, pray for us sinners,
now and at the hour of our death.
Amen.

I was a little surprised to get a call from Nicole, my bouncy, younger-by-six-years sister; I hadn't seen or heard from her in nine years. The last time we were together was when I was fifteen years old. On top of that, her offer was kind of a surprise. Our oldest sister, Michelle, who had been the rock of our family, at least to me in many ways, had received a honeymoon package to Punta Cana in the Dominican Republic; that was the only thing our estranged natural father had ever done for her. Michelle's husband was afraid to fly, so Michelle offered Nicole and me a honeymoon journey of our own.

I thought it was an amazing chance to bond with a sister I hardly knew so I accepted. We would share the honeymoon room — hopefully it had two beds —and just relax, get to know one another, and be treated well.

The Dominican Republic had a history for us girls. We had lived there as small children. I was born in Miami, a Cuban American, but went to the Dominican Republic when I was three. At the time, our mother, who had chosen to leave our father, decided to take the five of us to the DR so she could go to medical school there. It would be much cheaper than going to school in the States, and at this point, she was virtually a single mother with four children. It was the right place to go. The Dominican Republic turned out to be where she met her second husband who was also in medical school. Nicole, among other children, was born on that island.

We eventually returned to the States when I was seven, so my mother could do her medical residency in Richmond, Virginia before we moved back to Miami. In many ways, the Dominican Republic was an early home for all of us.

There had been a lot of pain during that time for our family, but I always believed in putting my best face forward and bringing positive energy to everything, no matter what happened. It seemed that Nicole felt the same way, and we both looked forward to this resort time by the sea. The past was the past. We were going to have a fun, beautiful time.

We both had seen more than our share of ugliness growing up, but God likes to play jokes, and the three of us girls were all blessed to look like angels who had grown up with harps playing around us, where everything was ribbons and bows. That was not at all the case.

Nicole is slender, blonde, and beautiful, a perfect purity in her looks. So, on day two of our "honeymoon," she was already dating the hotel manager (she was nineteen, after all). I was off men—I had too much history—and I just wanted to laugh, eat, drink, chill, and get to know my little sister.

Nicole has always been the life of the party. I am slightly more introverted, although I can act as though I am not. On this trip, I was a bit like her audience. But I am also friendly, so every day we met new people. I was twenty-five and Nicole was nineteen, as I said. We were magnets for attention from men.

As we lay on the beach, the palm trees moving gently around us, Nicole asked, "Aimee, don't you like any of these guys we keep meeting?" "No," I said, eyes closed, listening to the waves crash. "What's wrong with them?" she asked.

"They're nice but… I am not so interested in just having a good time." God knows I had been used enough for other people's good time.

"What kind of guy do you want to meet or be with?" she asked. Looking back, I see that she may have been trying to learn about life. After all, I was the older sister.

"I don't know. He has to have a good heart, be very intelligent, tall, great-looking –"

She laughed, "Make it easy, why don't you." "Oh," I added, "I would like if he were a doctor."

We had grown up around doctors, so this was not a vague request. Medicine had been part of our lives, so I knew what to expect with that life. I, myself, was studying to be a nurse.

We lay quietly in the sun for a bit, then… "Do you want to get married?" she asked.

"I pray for it all the time. I don't want to be lonely. I always pray that God removes any darkness around me and fills my soul and life with love. After all, I have been a single mother for seven years."

Nicole was just now learning how religious I was – and am.

I believe in God so I was pretty sure that one day my prayers would be answered. But I was also aware of the saying that God laughs while you are making plans. It wasn't like I was going around picking out wedding dresses, but this time He wasn't laughing.

It was the last night before we were to go home from our week- long sister honeymoon. Nicole, the manager, and I went to a club to celebrate our departure. The hotel manager invited his friend, Dr. Vaises, who brought along another doctor friend, Dr. Boris.

Dr. Boris turned out to be from Bulgaria and had wanted to leave his country during the post-communism struggle. Jobs there paid very little and there was much confusion on how to operate in a capitalist system. While he was making up his mind about what his next steps would be, he had found a job in the DR as the resort doctor. I thought I heard he also rotated to other hotels in Punta Cana. It sounded like a nice job if you could get it, although I would learn it was low-paying work.

Dr. Boris was making jokes with Dr. Vaises and casting curious and gentle looks at me. I was doing the same to him. He was tall and slender, and he had an unusually handsome boyish face, with dark laughing eyes. He was wearing glasses that gave him an intelligent look. But what struck me most was how polite he was with everyone. He was funny and interested in what other people were saying.

He came over to where I was sitting and asked Nicole and me about ourselves.

"We live in Miami," I said, smiling. This man simply made me light up. I told him I was in school pursuing medicine and that my mother was a doctor. So was my stepfather, but I left that out for the time being.

He was intrigued by this medical family. "So, you know what we go through?" he asked, teasing.

"I do," I laughed. "Especially the fake illnesses."

He said, "Older lonely rich women get a lot of those down here."

I laughed and replied, "I bet."

"I don't heal them," he explained. "Don't get that idea."

He seemed sincere. "Let me get both of you some more drinks," he said and went to the part of the bar where he could order.

I turned to Nicole, "This, this is one I could like."

"I just knew you'd find someone," she said, hugging me. But as he stood at the bar, another woman came up to him for a little private discussion, and I had a feeling that it wasn't about medicine. Well, men… we know how they are.

Nicole and I left the bar to go to the dance floor and I decided to forget him. *This place is a playboy's paradise*, I thought. *I don't need those problems.*

When we came back to the bar, Dr. Boris immediately came over and sat next to me, and for the rest of the night, he never left that seat. He joked with us and had us all laughing. He and I talked about our lives. We seemed to want the same things; we both planned to move up in the world, and neither of us was averse to working for it. He was thoughtful as he spoke, and I was shocked that I felt like I was falling in love. I would look at him, he would give me an encouraging, attentive grin, and my heart would soar toward him. I could see that he had a big soul.

Keep sane here, I said to myself. *We are flying back to Miami tomorrow.*

"Nicole," he said to my sister, "can I borrow your roommate for the evening? What time shall I return her for the flight?"

"Bring her home around six am, but make sure she is still a virgin."

He laughed. "I will," he promised.

I smiled, a bit embarrassed. How could I have such strong feelings for a man I had just met?

Nicole, the hotel manager, and Dr. Vaises left, and we continued to drink and talk quietly. Dr. Boris, whom everyone called Bobby, kissed me at the bar, and I thought, *Uh oh, I am in trouble.* The bar closed at two am and we went down to the basement where the hotel had given him an efficiency apartment. We continued kissing. Our attraction was on fire, but I broke away and said, "Bobby, you are wonderful. I prayed for someone like you, but I am not ready to get all involved and have a broken heart as I leave. We have to slow this down."

"What would you like then?" he asked, gently. There was no pushiness; he backed off right away, a gentleman. It was like a salve to my heart.

"A backrub!"

"A backrub?" he repeated, a little stunned. "A backrub."

Okay, that was going to torture him a bit; even I know I have an excellent shape. God had blessed me with a beautiful body, and I did my share of dancing and exercise. *Boris might as well know that the goods are top quality!* I kept my bra and panties on, and he gave me a backrub that, in and of itself, was almost more intimate than making love. He was giving to me, as opposed to taking. I was moved. Maybe it had been a test on my part, one that he passed with so much kindness and sensitivity; a doctor knows his anatomy after all. When we were finished, we talked more about our lives. He was the doctor on call, and he told me about the crazy "emergencies" he got —men who had been slashed by jealous wives, golf clubs in the wrong places, men who took too much Viagra that nothing would go down and, Bobby laughed, "That hurts." It was wild stuff. The backrub had relaxed me and soon we just fell asleep in each other's arms.

I felt complete, like this was where I was supposed to be; I did not want to be anywhere else. I could have stayed in those moments with him forever, but all too soon the alarm rang: six am. He sweetly walked me to the honeymoon room. We were close and romantic and then I said goodbye, forgetting that we had not exchanged any personal information. So much else had been going on between us. I was so excited just being with him that I almost didn't believe I was leaving. In a way, it felt like he and I were both in eternal time, but of course, I was leaving. *Get real here, Aimee. You will be in Miami later today.* Maybe I felt he could track me down if he wanted to, or felt he could, through the hotel manager knowing my sister.

Nicole and I went to the airport, and she peppered me with questions. "Did you?"

"No."

"Did you have a great time?" she asked.

"It was perfect." It went on and on until we were standing in front of the American Airlines agent.

"You look happy," the agent, a dark-haired older woman, said to me.

"Yes, but my sister made me realize I did not give the man of my life my number or address. I am crazy. Can you believe I met the man of my dreams," I explained to her (Who doesn't like to hear a love story?), "and now I will never see him again. I am such an idiot."

The agent looked at her screen and began typing. I kept feeling that I had missed an incredible moment. How could I have been so stupid!

Then the agent looked up and handed me a ticket. "It's for tomorrow. One for you and one for your sister. Go back and tell him where you live. No charge for the ticket change."

"Oh, my God, thank you!" I screamed. Nicole laughed and blew the agent kisses. We both ran out of there, almost dancing and shaking our heads at this miracle. As we got in the cab back to the hotel, I thought that God must approve of this man. He's trying to help make it happen.

Nicole was delighted to have an extra free vacation day and texted her hotel manager that we were on our way back. The manager must have found Bobby, and by the time we got to his place, the manager opened the car door and, on my side, guess who opened the door with a welcoming and sweet smile? Luckily, there were no emergencies at the hotel that day! We drank and talked, and I felt God loved me. This time I felt ready to make love with Bobby. *He can have any woman and he must know I care.*

I was a little insecure, thinking, *what will happen? Am I good enough?* Is this a one-night stand or is he really the one? But I put all that aside. When you love, you have to silence those negative voices and go toward the other person. That is the gift you are giving. When we were in his apartment that night, I said, "I have to tell you something. I have a little daughter, Danielle. She is my life. We have always been together, just the two of us."

"That's beautiful," he said. I showed him a picture. "Yes, she's as beautiful as you are."

"This time, we have to stay in touch," I said. "Although you don't know what you're getting into."

He laughed. "I can handle it." Then he hesitated and suddenly asked, "Why? Are you married?"

"No, not at all," I laughed.

"Good," he said and pulled me into his arms. And that night I made love to him like making love is supposed to be. I would trust him, I decided. Nicole and I flew back the next day, and that night he called me. He would do so every night until I saw him the next month when he flew me down to the DR for seven days. I knew I had met the man of my life.

So now my ritual was to put Danielle to bed and talk to Bobby for an hour before I went to bed. I was all too aware that other women must be coming on to him, with the alcohol and holiday atmosphere down there. Doctors at my school were coming on to me. Would we survive a long-distance relationship? Even more importantly, would he still respect and accept me once he knew me?

I wasn't perfect. I had been through some hard times, very hard times. I had been through events that I knew could ruin a person, and many people said that I had been ruined by these events. But I didn't believe it and I kept to my truth, knowing God's love kept me going. But I didn't know how Bobby would respond to my past, a past so horrific that it had made national news. During one of our calls, I said to him, "I hope you can love me. Everything is not always so rosy, you know." "Oh, come on," he said, "Why wouldn't I love you?"

Well, he was about to find out if he truly meant what he said. I began telling him the story.

Chapter 2

When I was three, my mother met three Cuban men in her medical school. One was David, a doctor who was tall and handsome like a Spanish Ken™ doll. David spent a lot of time with us, and my mother got pregnant with him. Their daughter was named Lisette, after my mother.

David was always nice to all of us, and we liked him. There were quite a lot of us kids. There was me, my older sister Michelle, two older brothers, and now this baby sister. But my mother was not sure about David. She had also met Antonio in school, and I guess he was not an issue. But then there was Andres, who was also tall and thin, with brown hair and a reddish-brown beard. Years later, I learned he was nineteen years old compared to my mother who was thirty at the time. Andres was also studying to be a pediatrician.

Andres started spending a lot of time around the house. My mother, still pregnant with Lisette, was going to have to make up her mind about who she should marry. In the meantime, my mother would sing to us. She had a beautiful voice. But even though she was young and pretty, she was juggling medical school and a gaggle of children. She had to be focused and almost militant about our lives. It was a lot to handle, and she was not studying to be a normal general practitioner, she was studying to be a neurologist. In addition, the Dominican Republic had its own challenges. As an example, we lived through three hurricanes, and twice we lost our house. I was too young to know how we managed, and all I remember is that she put us all on top of a table to keep us dry, trying to calm us down, as the table began to float in the flood.

She and David had to find a new home for us to live in when we lost our home. Through it all, though, we had fun as children in the Dominican Republic where there were lots of holidays. We would ride in a jeep and throw flour at the police officers chanting, "Policia pata podría dame un chele para la comida." (Translation: "Rotting leg Policemen, give me a cent for food.")

One night, we were all sitting around the table and my mother asked, "Whom should I marry? Andres or David?" This is a subject that kids love to make decisions about! All the other kids' hands shot up to vote for David. He was the fun one. Andres was quieter, more acquiescent to her.

"What about Andres?" she asked, laughing. I was the only one to raise my hand. I felt sorry for him. Nobody loved him. Somebody had to vote for him. He was the underdog, which was a little bit how I felt, being a middle sister. Strangely -- and she probably knew all along whom she wanted to marry, she married Andres. He joined our family, which was now four children whom she'd had with my biological father (whom we never saw) and Lisette, with David. It was interesting that my mother chose Andres since she had the more aggressive personality. He was more passive, but maybe she thought he would be easier to handle as she was already contending with so many children. My mother went on to have three more children with him: Nicole, Daniel, and Adrienne. Andres, her new husband, was the only man I ever remember calling *Papi*, the only father any of the children ever knew. In fact, I believed he was somehow my father. He was sweet to me and seemed to favor me.

While they were all in medical school, Andres' brother came to visit, and Andres and his brother decided to practice a physical exam on me. When they began talking about the hips, I felt uncomfortable. Andres had pulled my panties too low, and I felt embarrassed.

When I turned seven, our large family moved to Richmond, Virginia, where my mother would do her residency. Michelle and I took care of the babies. We didn't see our oldest brother, Jesusito, because he was in the army. When he came home, he was not friendly. He would chase me to beat me with a stick, and I would climb up a tree to get away from him. My mother, in turn, would sometimes chase him with a broom.

Michelle, my older sister, was sweet and loving. My mother had named her Michelle La Perfecta. She would cook for us, lookafter us, and keep the house tidy, but eventually, she ran away. I did not know why. She was fourteen at that time, and I was just seven. Maybe she no longer wanted to be the house mother. It just didn't make sense since Michelle was kind and not the type to abandon us. Without Michelle, we were alone a lot, since my mother's residency required her to work long hours. We were not completely alone, though, because Andres had not passed his exam and had to retake it. He was often home studying while my mother was working as a neurologist. Soon after we arrived in Richmond, I noticed that when I urinated, it stung and burned. I was sitting on the toilet and my mother came in.

"Why are you crying when you go to the bathroom?" she asked, in a clinical voice. She was trying to figure out if I was sick. Little did she know that she was looking for sickness in the wrong person.

I told her, "Papi rubbed his fingers too hard back and forth on my pipi." I was swollen and red.

My mother listened and then said, "I see."

The next thing I knew she took my Papi into the bedroom and locked the door. All of us children could hear her screaming, and shortly after, my dad came out with torn clothes and said, "What I did was wrong, and I am going to go away for a while to get help."

I really didn't understand that what Andres had done was not right, so I felt guilty to see him go. He was the one person who would listen to my stories and encourage me. I felt loved by him. In fact, he was kind to all of us, and when he was leaving all the kids were crying. I felt even more guilty now. After all, he was my best friend since my mother was never home. And when she was home, she had three little ones to take care of, so she hardly noticed me. And now I had made the whole family unhappy. *I shouldn't have opened my mouth*, I thought. *How could I have hurt him like this?* I told God I would never hurt anyone intentionally again. He hadn't done anything so terrible and now look what had happened. Now, we were going to be even more alone.

I had an interesting dream at this time. A monstrous bull, sent by the devil, came charging at me. Behind me was a small, fragile wooden doghouse. I knew the doghouse could not stand up against this bull and instead, I decided to kneel in front of it because I knew that if I sought shelter within the house, it would just fall to pieces once the bull charged. I had a lot of faith, and I remembered my mother saying, "If you seek God, He will help you." So, in my dream, I got down on my knees and asked God to save me. The bull, his nostrils fuming and his horns large and scary, was now coming at me with all his power. I knew my hideout would shatter but I did not give up hope and I prayed fervently. That's when the bull stopped in front of me and lay down to go to sleep. A gloomy sky lit up, and from the Heavens above, the most beautiful Jesus I ever saw descended to earth, accompanied by millions of angels dressed in white and singing the most glorious hymn of praise. It was when Jesus' feet touched the ground that little children appeared around me, laughing, happy children who quickly ran to hug Jesus.

Eagerly I said, "God, what about me?"

Jesus responded, "Come to me, my child." And I hugged Him, feeling mostly ribs. This dream was soothing, and I would wake up thinking, *I can always turn to God. I can depend on him.* It was as if He was watching over me, assuring me, "Don't worry, you are safe." But I didn't know the devil was about to send that bull my way.

Chapter 3

I'm stronger because I have to be. I'm smarter because of my mistakes.
I'm happier because I have overcome the sadness
I've known and I'm wiser because I have learned from my life.
Keep looking up to God for all things. **Adapted from Anonymous**

Two hours later, although it seemed like days to me, our dad returned home, and no one made any more mention of the fight. It was as if it had never happened. It was the same with his behavior. He continued touching me when my mother and siblings were not around and, because he was the only one I received love from, this time I knew to keep quiet. My school reported that I was a good actress, so good that I had been awarded a scholarship to a special acting school, an award only one student can win and this I earned after one rehearsal! It shows how well I was studying acting at home, where the role I played was docile, quiet, and accepting!

Maybe my acting award also showed how much I wanted to be another person. My mother did not respect actors and she thought that I would starve if I chose this career path, so I did not go to that school. We all did what she said, because if you didn't, and your grades were low, you got a beating. I continued my starring role of keeping to myself in the family and trying to be invisible.

I prayed a lot and had icons of God and the Virgin Mary on my bedroom wall. I believed that my previous dream was a promise from God that I would have the strength to handle whatever He sent my way. I now knew that what Andres was doing had to be kept secret. I did not quite understand it, but I knew enough. Conversely, he did know it was wrong, but that didn't stop him.

Interestingly, our handsome family of eight children and two doctor parents were featured in the Richmond newspaper as an example of success. My mother was pregnant with her ninth child, Adrienne. To the outside world, we looked like the perfect forward-moving, upstanding, intelligent, and committed family. When I was almost twelve, my mother finished her residency and we all moved back to Miami.

Miami was home in our hearts and this move was wonderful. The sea, the sun, and all the many Cubans who lived there made us feel that we fit into the landscape as easily as if we were beach pebbles. Andres had still not gotten his pediatrics license, so he was the home caretaker. We did not know my mother's family, her siblings, or her parents, so we were self-contained as a family unit. We did visit Andres' family in New Jersey a few times and these were typical Cuban get-togethers. Kids, more kids, and a lot of food. Normal life. At home, this was not the case.

We were not allowed to have friends come over, but there were so many of us kids that we were able to hold our own Olympics in our backyard. Since Michelle had already run away, I was the oldest girl, and I was starting to be a little more vocal. My oldest brother never returned home from the army, so it was just us younger ones. I had a brother, Javier, one year older than me, and we were now sworn enemies, as pre-teenagers can be. His method of attack was to tattle on me. If I sat next to a boy on the school bus, he would immediately tell my mother and I would get a beating.

Any maid my mother hired could not handle the kids and the house, so the house was always dirty. I was in charge of cleaning since I was the oldest girl, and if the house wasn't clean, I got a beating. These beatings were not spankings. My mother would use a belt on me, and one time she even broke a hole in the wall from banging my head against it. Perhaps she felt she could do neurosurgery on my head if she broke it.

My father, Andres, would scream, "Stop it, Lisette. You're going to kill her."

I would go to my room crying. Then he would come in and close the door. "Don't worry, honey. I know you are trying to help her. Let me see those welts."

I would cry harder, becoming almost hysterical, and he would say, "Aimee, you are the special one. Even though you try to hide when she gets home, everyone can see you are beautiful and perfect."

"She is an ogre," I said. "She used to be nice."

"She has many responsibilities, but you, Aimee," he'd say stroking my back and smiling reassuringly at me, "are sweet and gentle. Keep your heart pure." And listening to this, I thought, *my Papi sees the real me. I have someone.*

June marked my twelfth birthday and Andres said, "I have a birthday present for you." He had come into my bedroom where I was supposed to be studying, but really, I was just hiding from the rest of the house.

"What?" I asked, excited. I sat up from my bed.

"I will take your virginity. If someone who loves you does it, it is much better than some clumsy stupid boy."

"I don't think so," I said, a little scared, my body on red alert. "No, I am right," he said and grabbed my arm. I pulled away but he fought me and pulled me toward him, overwhelming me physically. He aggressively pulled off my t-shirt as I struggled. He slapped me to stop me from pushing him away and then pulled down my jeans and panties, holding my arms behind my back. He pushed me down on the bed and held my arms in a tight grip over my head as I lay on the bed. He then pushed himself into me which hurt, but I was used to pain. *My mother has seen to that with her punishments*, I thought as he pumped away. I stared at the ceiling and told myself, *well, he can't help it. He really loves me. I will just put up with this.*

Then he began visiting my room daily. He took the opportunity to rape me when my mother was at work, which seemed to be all the time since she worked at several hospitals and had her own medical office. He would start slowly and touch me gently and then he would get overwhelmed and get on top of me and enter me.

Sometimes he wanted oral sex which always made me gag and feel sick. Other times he would try to put the bristles of a round-brush into my vagina, which of course did not fit. And, looking back, I cannot imagine why he would do this. It shows that rape is more about power than eroticism.

During all of this, I would stare numbly at the ceiling, imagining I was far away. *Is this the price of someone loving you? Do you have to do what they want? And it doesn't matter how you feel?* Afterward, I would sit in my closet and imagine getting beamed up to another reality where nothing mattered, and I was with God, and everything was fine. Even my brother Javier tried to have sex with me, but I was able to get away from him by refusing his advances. Then Andres' younger brother, Rafael, came to stay and one afternoon he just came into the bathroom when I was washing my hair. He blocked me as I tried to get out of the bathroom, turned me around, pulled my pants down, and raped me from behind, never saying a word. I went numb, once again, knowing it would be over in minutes, which it was. Neither of us ever said a word to each other again.

After he walked out, I told myself, *these people are all like that; they can't help it. I will be the bigger person and act normal. I will get through this by not getting upset. I will ignore it.* I didn't want to say anything because I did not want to cause a disruption as I had when I was seven. I did not even tell Andres about what his brother had done to me.

What I did was keep a coded diary, but I was so secretive that I never wrote explicitly about the abuse. Even though I kept it in code, I knew that Javier was an expert spy and that they would eventually find my code. He had the idea that the more he got me in trouble, the more my mother would love him. Now I know this means that he did not feel loved either.

When I was fourteen, Andres began accosting me in the maid's bathroom, saying, "You've been a bad girl. You need to be punished." This meant sudden anal sex, his new preference. It hurt horribly but I had to be quiet so no one would hear. Sometimes, I would hold my breath to help with the pain, only later to find myself bleeding. The pain became part of my body that I felt constantly. I would cry from the pain but only let myself feel it quickly or secretly so that no one would find out why I was crying.

My mother kept on with her beatings that occurred on an almost daily basis, since I was always in trouble in her opinion. Javier told her, once again, that I had kissed a boy on the bus, so she cut my hair super short to look like a boy's. Now, not only was I in physical pain, under attack, and silenced, which can make you feel ugly on the inside, but I also felt ugly on the outside. No one would want to be my friend.

Did my mother unconsciously suspect what Andres was doing and want to punish me? Did she see him looking at me and hate me for that? Andres was very free with the way he went after me in front of my mother. One time, I was sitting on her bed talking to her. She liked me to give her a type of back rub where I tickled her back. She would lie on her side, with her back turned to me and Andres would appear out of nowhere and penetrate me with his finger while I was on my side facing my mother's back. He would lie down facing my back. I remember thinking, *wow, he is really gutsy*. It would make me nervous, and

I would freeze, hoping my mother wouldn't know what was going on. *How could she not know? What was she thinking when he was on the bed with us, and she heard her husband's breathing and the silence?* But, like everything else at that point in my life, I could not think about this reality, let alone face it.

At this time, Javier was also getting beaten, but Andres was doing these beatings. Andres once held my brother's head down in our filthy pool before the water had been changed. My mother did not beat Javier as much since he was her vehicle for getting bad information about me. But Javier must have been frightened of them both, because once he walked in on Andres and me. I was completely naked, lying down on Andres' lap. Andres pushed Javier away and shut the door. In spite of his role as the house spy, Javier said nothing, perhaps fearing Andres in this case. I told myself, *just pray and get through this.* At this point, my mother decided that Javier and I should be home schooled to keep me away from boys. This was the height of irony. I would be even more available to her husband.

She was going to be the one to teach us, but since she was never at home, I never went beyond seventh grade at that time. Even my mother knew she was being horrible, so sometimes she would take me on her hospital rounds. I would feel proud of her. Everyone looked up to her. The nurses were conversational and attentive to me, complimenting me when I was there, something I was not used to.

I decided I would be a doctor, too, or a saint. My mother had me read the books of Saint Padre Pio and Saint Dominic Savio, a child saint. Saint Padre Pio had bad table manners and fought the devil every night, a little like what I was going through in my house, but Saint Dominic Savio was tough enough to win. If he could survive, then I could, too. My mother was always saying that if we lied, God would reveal the truth to her when she read the Bible. She felt children were innocent until they were seven and, after that, they were not to be trusted. I thought she might kill me if she found out what Andres was doing to me, but I also thought that I wouldn't mind dying —I would be with God, even if she was the bull to shatter my house. And maybe she was. She should have been protecting me.

No one knew what was going on, not even the people in the same house. But something was going to have to give. That much was clear.

Chapter 4

God, I know You are able to heal me in every way. I need healing—mentally, emotionally, spiritually, physically… And I know it is Your will to heal me because Your son died so that I could be healed. God, let the beauty of His sacrifice sink into my spirit and fill me with faith to trust in Your Word.
I ask You for healing right now.
Wash me clean from the inside out and fill me with Your love and righteousness. God, I reject every doubt in my mind that sets itself up against Your Word, and I accept Your gift of healing.
Above all things, I trust in You. **Joyce Meyer**

I was fifteen years old when my older sister Michelle returned home. She had been staying in New Jersey with Nadia, a friend of our mother. Before that, she had stayed with Chris, one of Andres' brothers; Chris had a sense of what was going on in our house because he had heard of such behavior by Andres with his own children. This brother had been sympathetic to Michelle.

Her coming home was odd since she was married to a man named Rick, had a baby, and they were living with Rick's parents. Either she was having trouble with Rick, or she missed the family; after all, she had taken care of us. We were like her children, and I believe she came back because she loved us. At that time, none of this was discussed. It was like Michelle was on a reconnaissance mission.

Whatever her reason, I was thrilled to have her back in the house. She was someone I knew I could trust and who would not hurt me.

She immediately began caring for us kids, cooking for us and generally being a wholesome addition to this very wounded family. But one day, I came into the kitchen and there was Michelle, frozen, and Andres, a big man, with his hand up her blouse, touching her breasts. I could feel the tension in the air. I turned around, heartbroken. It wasn't that Andres was touching my sister and not me; I was used to his behavior. Not for a minute did I have any feelings that he belonged to me. After all, he was married to my mother and went to bed in her bedroom each night. I was sick that Michelle, whom I looked up to and was an idol of mine, had to go through this, too.

The next night, I wasn't surprised when I walked into her room and she was furiously packing her things. Once again, I was going to be left in this horrible house where I was under constant sexual attack.

"Don't go," I said. "Please. I can't be here alone."

I still remember being somewhat surprised by the streetlight next to our house flashing red, when it normally flashed yellow. Was this a sign?

I said, "Take me with you. Please. I don't care where you are going."

She had tears in her eyes, as she kept throwing things in a bag. "Why are you going anyway?" I asked.

She just looked at me and wouldn't answer my question. It was too sad for her. She must have been feeling tremendous disappointment and heartbreak of her own about what was going on in our house. She now knew the irrevocable truth. She looked at me for a few seconds and then finally spoke.

"Why do YOU want to run away?" she asked. And then I blurted it all out, and it was the first time, since I was seven years old, that I had spoken to anyone about what was going on there. I told her everything. Andres. Rafael. All of it. The daily anal sex. The pain. The beatings from our mother. Not going to school. All of it.

"I can't go through it anymore," I said, crying. "I have to leave. This is hell, Michelle. I am in hell here. I will die if I stay." Michelle listened and I could see her thinking. I stood there in terrible grief, and I could see her make a decision. She grabbed me and said, "Let's go."

"Where?"

"Just come with me."

We ran out of the house. I followed her, and I could hardly breathe but I was getting away. Then, I saw she was leading us to the neighbors' house. I hadn't expected this. I didn't know the neighbors very well. They were a middle-aged couple, very quiet, and studious. They minded their own business.

Michelle said to them, "Excuse me, but we need your phone, please."

"Of course," the woman said. She might have known that our house was a place of trouble. She might have heard the crying and the beatings. I stood there waiting to see who Michelle would call. She called the police. The next thing I knew, a detective was there, a female detective, Ellen Christopher. There were other police, and a social worker, even though it was late at night. They must have heard in Michelle's voice that this was no small family argument. They must have heard that this was the real thing. The detective sat down with me and said, "Tell me what is going on."

I was so ashamed that I could not look her in the eye. "My Papi is having continual sex with me, forced sex, and I cannot take it anymore." She asked me more questions and I had to describe it. All of it. It was humiliating and terrifying.

"Does anyone know?" she asked.

"No," I said. "I only keep a diary under my bed." I forgot to tell her it was coded but she rushed across the street to our house to look for my diary. Now I understand that she saw it as proof if we got into legal issues.

She came back. "There is nothing about abuse in here," she said.

"It is in code because I did not want them to read it. My brother Javier likes to spy on me."

She looked suspiciously at me. "You realize if what you are saying is true, your father Andres will go to jail. And all the kids will be taken away from your parents. Do you want this?"

I had done it again. I had gotten him in trouble. I was ruining the family with my mouth. Regardless of what was being done to me, I loved my parents. This is, as some may already know, common for abused children.

I felt sick. I said, "I will kill myself if my father goes to jail."

"You will what?"

"Kill myself."

The detective looked at me in disgust. I do not think she believed the extent of the abuse I had been going through or that I would kill myself. I probably would not have killed myself, on account of my religious beliefs, but I could see she thought I was crazy. Michelle also saw her distrust of me and said, "My sister is telling the truth because I have lived through some of this myself." The detective and the police had to act on that statement or they themselves would be violating the law.

"You must take the kids from that house and save them," Michelle said.

"Where will they go?" the social worker asked.

"They can live with me. I will take them to where I have a place with my husband's in-laws and then we will get a bigger place and they can be with me. They are used to me taking care of them."

"Why did you go home if you have a husband?" asked the detective.

"I wanted to see what was going on and how the kids were faring."

I could see the detective and social worker conferring. Michelle stood up tall and was adamant. "There is non-stop abuse in that house," she said. "Lots of it. You must believe it and have the other kids removed or more terrible things will happen. I couldn't just turn a blind eye."

The detective listened, then said, "I would like to confer with Ms. Meredith, the social services lady." They went into another room at the neighbor's house and the detective closed the door behind her. The neighbor had tactfully removed herself and she was sitting in the living room. The policemen were taking calls on walkie-talkies and waiting to be told what to do next, so they could go to their next call. Michelle held my hand. We waited. The detective came out and called in the police officers, they talked, and then the officers and the detective and social worker left. Michelle and I were told to wait at the neighbors' house. We waited and the neighbor kindly gave us something to eat. I remember being surprised there were empanadas since empanadas are South American. It made me feel somehow like everything would be alright. Less than two hours later, seven police officers removed all the children from my parents' home and came to get Michelle so she could take them to her other home.

"Not her," the detective said looking at me. "Why?" Michelle and I asked bewildered.

"When someone mentions suicide, they must be hospitalized," the detective said. "It is a law. We need to take her to Jackson Crisis Center. They will attend to her psychologically and then we can see what should happen next."

The police and other kids were outside, and Michelle had to go; we all had to act fast, and she hugged me and said, "Don't worry."

The social worker gestured to me and said, "I will go with her." I was scared and tired and drained, but I also knew I was on my way out of that house. I was not going back. Never. And I was used to being alone. Whatever was going to happen, and wherever it was going to happen, seemed to me to be a type of improvement.

Chapter 5

Let God's strength be perfected on your weakness.
He uses our brokenness to rebuild us so we are stronger.
You're never too imperfect for GOD! **from 2 Corinthians 12:7-10**

They give you a lot of drugs in the hospital and, as patients, we would sit in front of the TV to pass the time. That's when I saw a very unusual star on the news.

"I am a leading Miami neurologist, and my husband is a respected pediatrician. This whole abuse of the child welfare services, where they come in on the word of two malicious sisters who are rebelling against a responsibly disciplined family life and convince the welfare services that my husband and I are abusive, so much so that my other children are taken away —this is proof of a criminal system. This may be some anti-Cuban, anti-Hispanic action on the part of social services," my mother continued. "But we will fight this injustice all through the courts. Let me assure you."

I just sat there crying. I knew that the courts were up against a force. Even though my mother might be neglectful, blind, and cruel, she was also a genius manipulator. I knew she was not averse to lying and making me look like the crazy one. I turned around and went to bed.

At the hospital, I would get visits from the guardian ad litem, Mrs. June Shaw. She was a very sweet older lady who genuinely seemed to care about me. She was my only visitor. I had my birthday in the hospital, and she was the only person who remembered it and brought me a little present. If my parents were telling the truth about being the loving responsible parents, wouldn't they have come?

It was cold in the hospital. We had to get up early and our days were filled with activities, in addition to individual and group therapy. I never spoke at all in group therapy, nor did I talk much in individual therapy. There was one nurse I liked. He seemed to know me best and didn't mind my silence. He would talk to me anyway.

"Boy, Aimee, the day you let that anger out, people better watch out! Don't get in a fight because you might really hurt someone. You are suppressing so much that when it comes up, man," he said, "you could kill someone." I thought this was an odd thing to say since I was so quiet. I was the last person to get into a fight. I remembered having been in one fight in my life.

It was at the beginning of the 7th grade when a tall black girl tried to take the seat I had chosen. Since it was "first come first serve" in the class, and I had arrived early, I wanted the front row to pay better attention, as I would get lost in my studies and the boy everyone liked sat behind me.

I had said to her, "This seat doesn't have your name on it." She started swinging punches. I was taking Kung Fu at the time, so I effectively blocked every punch. She couldn't even touch me, and I did not try to hit her back. I just blocked and blocked for about three minutes until the teacher walked in.

"What's going on?"

"Nothing," we both answered. But I kept the seat. I was never one to slink away. I've always been a fighter but only in self-defense. As it turned out, my adversary respected me and later became my friend. The friendship didn't last long though; soon after, my brother and I began being home schooled. In truth, though, I am a born peacemaker, and even the girl at school and I quickly got to that place. I also knew that if my anger ever got to be too much, I was more likely to take it out on myself, not someone else. I was the one who deserved it, I thought, because I was always creating a mess. There were lawsuits everywhere, according to the news, and once again, I had broken up the family.

I saw many psychiatrists and I could tell them what had happened to me with Andres, but I could not access any feelings. I felt nothing at all, just hatred for myself. I missed my brothers and sisters, but at this point I believed I didn't deserve even them, especially since I was the whistle-blower. I'd lie on my bed and think, *why could I not keep quiet? Why was I not strong enough to tolerate Andres and my mother any longer? Why didn't I find a different way to run away?* I felt I had shattered my own family. One day I sneaked a look at one of my reports while I was waiting to be seen in therapy. There, in shrink language, it said, "There is basically no hope for her. It is too late." *Maybe they are right,* I thought. *Maybe they are wrong.*

The case was now high profile, and it was being talked about all over the news, thanks to my mother's vehemence to prove herself innocent. My mother had only terrible things to say about Michelle and me. Michelle was a sociopath who wanted her money. I apparently followed along because I wanted freedom from a restrictive house. She said I had a twenty-eight-year-old boyfriend and that was why I wanted out. In truth, I had only seen this man twice. She said that I had already told a friend that I had lied. This was not true, but it made for a good story.

She never questioned her husband's abuse.

Shelly Snodgrass, the children's and family worker now in charge of what was to happen to me, had a passion for helping and protecting children. She wasn't falling for my mother's puffed-up righteousness. Shelly was super cool, with a wavy hairstyle that was similar to mine and she believed in me. I felt that she was a guardian angel sent to protect me. Shelly explained to me that my mother was now taking legal action to win her case and get all the children back. She had ordered a judge to assign a set of psychological tests for Michelle and myself. Sadly, for my mother, we were found to be sane. My mother then hired another psychologist of her own whom she hoped to influence. He also determined that we were sane, and he also apparently made her take some tests and found out that she was brilliant, a genius, but that she had symptoms of grandiosity. Michelle joined forces with Shelly and June Shaw and Attorney Robin Greene, who was tough as nails, to fight my mother and ensure that I would not have to go back, nor would any of the other children. They were a great, strong team, but they were up against formidable odds.

Featured in the *Miami Herald* and the *Miami New Times*, my mother loved the drama of it, and she was getting more creative about her claims against my sister Michelle, stating Michelle was a narcissist, a histrionic sociopath with Munchhausen syndrome by proxy, who was not only after her parent's money but was also out for personal fame. My mother stayed with her original story about me: I played along, she said, because I wanted freedom from a strict environment. But she managed to get the reporters who listened to her to interpret me as being unstable and untruthful. Since I was staying in a psychiatric facility, perhaps people believed her. In a way, I distanced myself from the whole thing. I just had to concentrate on fighting a type of PTSD every day. Articles began to appear, and this case was named "The Case from Hell." In that, they were not wrong. It was heart-breaking to now be pitted against my mother and to see she did not care about my feelings or what had happened to me. There are some people who would rather be proven right— even when they are wrong—than come to a loving solution.

Meanwhile, I was still deemed in psychological danger of suicide, so I was moved to another psychiatric hospital, Grant Central Psychiatric Hospital for Adolescents. I stayed in that hospital for six weeks. Really, they were stalling for time to figure out where they were going to send me. No one wanted to send me home, and I didn't want to go either. Everyone was lawyering up and Janet Reno was about to get involved. These three women who were my advocates were making me feel less helpless, and it was a wonderful thing to have adults around me who were not interested in abusing me. I was not unhappy in the hospital. It was the first time in my life that I was not being used. But it was not the last time in my life that I would have to face abuse. That bull with the devilish eyes had not finished with me yet.

Chapter 6

In order to go to the next level, we must ignore ignorance,
neglect negativity, and disregard disrespect.
Success isn't for the weak. **Anonymous**

B
obby and I had been talking on the phone every night since my return from the Dominican Republic. We would laugh, share music, and tell each other everything. If it is possible to be in love after one night and thirty phone calls, that was what we were. A month after we met, he wanted me to come back to the Dominican Republic to visit him. I wanted to go too, so I let Danielle stay with her father. I could only stay a week with Bobby because I was in school, and I was dedicated to getting my degree. Getting a degree was incredibly important to me since it was one way I could prove to the world that I was a healthy, productive person for my daughter. I was not going to mess with that. At all. Yet I was about to go see the man whom I felt was the first good man I had ever met. I had met all too many men who were anything but that. But what if he turned out to be like them? What if I was misjudging him as I had misjudged so many others, as victims of abuse often do? It's like men can smell that you have been a victim and they think they'd like to pick you off, too. So, as much as I loved every conversation and moment with Bobby, I was scared. *Could I really trust this?*

I did what I always do when scared, I prayed: *Dear God, You know what I've been through with men. I even thought about being gay, but it isn't in me. But, even so, I want to find someone good: a partner, a husband. I am tired of struggling alone with my daughter; it feels like it's me against the world. I don't want to risk her having to spend an entire week with her father, whom I don't have much good to say about, for a long-distance relationship that goes nowhere. Please God, give me a sign that this is all worth it, that I am not once again getting myself into something terrible. I don't want any more men who are only out for themselves. Make this a man I can marry. I've asked You to choose my husband, and if he is the one, please let me know with a sign. I will tell You the sign I want —for Bobby to propose to me, even though I know this is only the second time I will see him. But I cannot go through any more pain. You know that. Thank You, God.*

And I got on the plane and thought, *I will explain to Bobby how I feel.* I mean, if I want to be with him, and I can't explain how I feel about who I am now, what good is it anyway?

He met me at the airport looking so handsome, his black-brown hair curly and full, his intense dark eyes shining and laughing. He wore a white shirt and jeans, and his warmth embraced me. He had planned our first night at a beautiful resort restaurant over the sea. There we were, smiling and happy to be together and I thought he was so beautiful, as were the moon on the sea, the salty air, the rustling of the trees, the friendliness of the waiters, and the freedom I felt just being with him. I thought I was in a dream, and for the first time, it was a good one. But I had to protect myself.

I smiled at Bobby, leaning forward. We were holding hands on the table. "Bobby," I said, "thank you for flying me here for seven days. I love being with you; I know that. You are so special, and I am so grateful to have met you. You are everything to me, but we cannot do what we did the second night I was with you." He listened attentively.

I continued, "I am very into God; I guess you know that already. And I am no virgin; you know that too, but I believe it is never too late to do the right thing. I want to be appropriate and get to know each other and be sure we really want to go forward together."

He listened, then said, "Go on."

"That's it. I think you should really know me, too, before... you know...before we... you know. I don't want a holiday romance. I want the real thing." I waited. This was where it would come clear. The men I had known never wanted to know me; they only wanted to know the lower half of my body. Bobby smiled mischievously. "Well," he said, "I have a solution to our problem."

"Yes?"

"Come with me," he said, suddenly standing up. "It's in the lobby of the resort. Don't worry, I am not taking you to a room. We can come back and finish our dinner after I show you."

"Okay."

I put my napkin down, put my foot back into one of my heels I had slipped off, and got up. Bobby extended his hand so that I would go first. He told the waiter, "We'll be right back," and then he put his hand on my back and walked me through the restaurant to the lobby to a small shop, a jewelry store in the hotel. *Oh, my God.*

He turned to me, "Would you like to pick your ring?"

I couldn't believe it. It was such a brave act for him to make —so sweet and intuitive. He knew my heart's desire and he was giving it to me. I didn't hesitate for a moment. I knew this God-given man was my soulmate, the only man I would ever marry. I didn't need time to figure that out. I hugged him and said, "Yes, I would." I quietly said to myself, *Thank You, God,* and I picked a small, elegant, solitary diamond.

It had to be sized, so after he paid for it, we went back to our table, glowing with our excitement. The waiters brought us champagne once we announced we were engaged, and the moon seemed even brighter, even through my occasional tears.

"I am so happy," I said. "I am too," he said.

When I thought about it, he was also alone. Here he was from Bulgaria, in the Dominican Republic, a place he probably never heard of when he was growing up, just to get away from a repressive regime, as I too had run away from a repressive and cruel regime in my own home. We would be a union of two people who had been very much on our own and who needed a home where we could thrive. *Our union,* I thought, *must have been meant to be.* We would join and make a family and life together.

I was elated. I was engaged to this angel and then he said, "You can always tell me everything. I want to know all of you. And I will always be there for you." I absolutely knew in my heart that he was telling the truth. He had shown that in the strength of his actions, actions that were only loving. True love makes you strong, it makes you willing to take risks, and his risks were ones that were based in love, not on using someone else. I was now with someone I could trust, who was non-judgemental, and who had opened my heart. I was a person who'd always hidden my pain and hidden my hand of cards, but I had also been given the gift of knowing that was no way of fostering a fulfilling life with someone. I knew that I had to risk being known, and if I risked it, he would feel the gift and responsibility of that trust because he was that kind of man. Something in me knew I had found my home, somewhere safe. That is what made me decide to tell him everything.

Over the next seven days, I continued recounting my story.

Chapter 7

You have to believe in yourself with everything that is within you, especially when
times get rough, and you want to question things.
That's when doubt begins creeping in.
Let people count you out if they want to consider you a non-factor; that's when you
rise from the ashes and take your lemons and make lemonade. **Aimee Cabo**

Now there were three power hitters representing me on "The Case from Hell": the soon-to-be US Attorney General, Janet Reno, who must have been advising my prosecuting family attorney Anita Boch, a witty, pretty lady with blonde hair. There was also a maverick attorney, Mark Schneider, who was a good-looking, tall German American whose job on my case was to take on the police and the media. This case was not really about the children at this point; it had become about legal technicalities and who was breaking what law. I didn't follow it for obvious reasons. I was removed from the world and depressed, and the entire case made me even more depressed.

The attorneys on the other side, under my mother's sort of magnificent influence, were doing everything to get the other children back. Michelle had no love for my mother and one side of the argument said Michelle was influencing the children to say terrible things about our mother. Lawyers, psychologists, and everyone legally involved had no idea of who was telling the truth. Even I did not know, because I was not there. The children were, of course, very young and malleable, except for Javier, who was under my mother's thumb. Javier was not living with Michelle; instead, he was living with my oldest brother. I am sure my younger siblings just wanted their mother back and did not want to be sent away. And I am also sure Michelle was forceful in stressing the risk of further abuses in the household.

The attorneys and mental health professionals began attacking each other over misuse of jurisdictions and withholding information from each other. This suspicion did not help anyone's case. What was difficult for me was that people believed me less and less, which is a different form of abuse. I knew what I had been through, but I was being talked about in the news —which I would intermittently watch —as though I were crazy. They called me a liar, sexually promiscuous, and untrustworthy. My own mother was calling me these things. It was no wonder that my depression was not lifting but maybe sinking deeper.

The media was having a field day. We all know how the media are not always so interested in the truth but more interested in drama. This drama was now affecting all the players and the truths of the case were being ignored for the glitzier issues of a long-suffering, hardworking mother being falsely accused by her devious children. It was an unusual twist. Usually, the grownups are the abusers, but somehow my mother had managed to build a case where the children were abusing the parents. It was a crazy premise, but crazy premises can be mesmerizing.

Even though my own family did not believe me, even though I could not rely on their care, and even though I had been physically, emotionally, and sexually abused by them for years, I now felt guilty again. By speaking up, I had split up the entire family and put everyone under the duress of having to choose sides. For what? For nothing. All the devilish players were still lying, still promoting their innocence, and it seemed like everything would continue as it had. People were believing my mother and Andres. I had changed nothing. There was only one change that everyone on my team was agreed upon: I could not go home. But after three months in two hospitals, my insurance must have run out. Now, what would they do with me?

It had not gone unnoticed by my team that this loving, long- suffering mother had never once visited me or called me to see how I was. Perhaps she was too angry that the other children had been taken away. Perhaps she was too angry that Andres had his pediatric license suspended. Or perhaps she just didn't care. But it was clear she chose to demonize her own child rather than bother to speak with me in person. The Department of Children and Families (then called HRS) found temporary housing for me in a foster home where I was the only Hispanic girl. I slept in a bunk bed, in a room full of kids, in a rundown house, in a ghetto. I heard shots in the middle of the night. I was elated when this stay only lasted for a weekend.

I was then taken to a long-term foster home and placed with a detective and his Christian wife; they were young and they had a nice clean house. There was some regularity in their lives. I was the only kid in the household, and at first, they seemed like the perfect couple. Dinner was on the table. They spoke to me politely. One morning, the wife went to church to sing in the choir. Her husband, Bob Maxwell, entered my room wearing only a robe, exposing his naked body, and he raped me.

It was happening again.

After that, my mind went numb. I blocked out the rest of my stay in their house. I felt I was doomed. *Why does this go on everywhere? Is this a plot to drive me crazy? Is there no one with whom I can ever feel safe?* This new betrayal was the end of my ability to feel. I just didn't care about life anymore. I went to more foster homes, but I could not bond. I hated homes and parental figures, and as soon as I could, I ran away to Miami Bridge, a runaway shelter, and lived with friends in low economic areas for a short while. I became a kind of vagrant, moving around and staying with different people.

I was, in a way, a fugitive, but it was better than living with untrustworthy adults. Jeanette, my mother's favorite, two years younger than me, also ran away from her upscale foster home, where she had been placed after refusing to live with Michelle. I would see her off and on as we traversed Miami, but in our own ways, we were both in shell shock and using every ounce of strength we had to keep our own selves together. We could not help each other much. She had been taught to distrust me. I was aware she had a bond with my mother, and maybe I feared that. Maybe having a bond with someone who was so cruel to me felt like a betrayal.

Even so, I was very young, and perhaps because of that, some hope still flickered in my heart. I had been deeply instilled with the belief that everyone is essentially good, as we are all made in Christ's image. Not everyone could be bad. Believing that, I walked among dark alleys and took a lot of risks by befriending dangerous people who themselves had been abused and had burned the sensitivity out of themselves. Drug dealers. Scammers. People who were just poor and had to do whatever they could to get by. Yet nothing scared me. I knew God was in control; I just didn't know why He wouldn't take my life. I was giving Him a lot of chances, although many, if not all, people treated me well. We were all people who had gone through hard times and there is, as they say, an honesty among thieves. There can be great kindness among those who are lost.

God seemed to have chosen such an odd path for me to walk. I did not consider suicide since my mother had convinced me that if one kills oneself, one automatically goes to hell.

It was interesting that the press referred to our case as "The Case from Hell," yet, I believed that if what I had been living was hell on earth, I imagined that a hell without God would have been worse. Once, two guys dared me to drink an entire bottle of MD 2020. I didn't like the taste of alcohol, but I always took pride in being tough. I was sixteen years old, and I thought I could handle anything. Up to this point, I had been handling everything and anything. I became inebriated and passed out. Once I came to for a short while, I awoke enough to hear them arguing about having their turn on me, complaining that the other one was taking too long. I was so drunk that they didn't even have to restrain me in any way. I was dizzy, asleep, and out of it. I didn't say anything when I finally came to, vomiting repeatedly. I just brushed it off and left, never thinking of it again or mentioning anything to anyone.

This was something that I was now used to; I believed I was already broken, and I didn't matter much. This seemed to be what God had given me to do. But I never spoke to them again.

I had to think, *why does this happen to me? Do I bring it about in any way?* I did not know that a young girl who has no sense of self and is pretty, just evokes a kind of predatory sexuality in men who are as weak themselves. I did not know or understand that then. But I was starting to fear that the abused goes for the abuse, and if this was true, what would my future be?

I knew God was helping me in some way because I never slept on the streets, and I never went hungry. At this time, my mother appeared. She had an injunction not to see the kids, but she had found out where Jeanette and I were and picked us up. I agreed to go with my mother because it couldn't get any worse than my present circumstances. Also, I still felt guilty from the ramifications of saying the truth. Now the three of us were fugitives from the law since none of us were supposed to be together. We kept changing hotels and even states to avoid being caught since there were investigators and police following the case. My mother talked me into writing out a fifty-page recantation letter that she would dictate. This letter was the only way she could get the children back. At this time, the police had gone to Andres to find out where we were. He would not tell them, so they put him in jail for obstructing justice.

I so much wanted my mother to love me that I could not think of my own story. I just felt badly that I had ruined her life by having the children removed. I also felt bad that I had seemingly made the children's lives unhappy by separating them from her (I did not think Andres was the same with the other children), so I agreed to the recantation.

In addition to the document I had to write, she also wanted me to take two lie detector tests, which I did in New York during our fugitive run. I had to take back everything I had ever said about what was done to me, affirm that my parents were not guilty of any wrongdoing, and validate my mother's assessment of my oldest sister Michelle as a sick person. I figured out how to lie on a lie detector test! I accelerated my breathing when I was asked to lie and remained calm when asked to say the truth at baseline.

This recantation letter was a tactic my mother had used before. She had made Michelle, when she was young, recant her claims against Andres for fondling her, but now Michelle refused to recant. Even so, my long recantation would be the lynchpin to help my mother get the children back. She let the press and her lawyers know what "I" had written. Michelle ended up keeping Nicole, who did not want to return to our parents, and Michelle raised her. The other children went home.

When we came back from our fugitive run, I lived with friends, and I decided to get a job. I thought a job would be a start toward something new and living a good life. I did not want to go home because of Andres. I began selling tickets at a movie theatre. The manager at my job was a handsome young man, Brent, who was good-looking, blonde, and blue-eyed, and we were immediately attracted to each other. I thought this must be a normal person with a job and his own home and his own dreams. I was tired of foster homes and being homeless, and I very much wanted a place to belong.

I quickly moved in with Brent, and now I had a real boyfriend. Living with Brent was indeed better than living at the Miami Bridge, but he started to become jealous and possessive, and when he was angry, he would hit me. I became pregnant within a few months of living with him, and he punched me right in the stomach, so I miscarried. You are probably thinking: why did I stay with him? Keep in mind that I thought I had nowhere else to go, and I had already been beaten as a child, so I was able to convince myself that Brent's behavior was somewhat normal. It would never have occurred to me that I might deserve better treatment. I had neither known nor ever seen better treatment anywhere.

But after eight months of living with Brent, I became pregnant again, and this time I knew I had to protect the unborn baby I was carrying. I decided to leave, but where was I going to go, pregnant and alone? I am religious and so, of course, I would not abort. I am against that. And I looked forward to my child. I had to give her all that I had not had myself. With her, I would no longer be alone, and she and I would rise above all this. But there was nowhere to go.

And what does a child do when they have nowhere to go and feel there is no one in the world to help them? I told my mother I wanted to come home and have my baby. My mother agreed on the condition that I would keep to my story that Andres was innocent. For the sake of my unborn child, I said, "Yes, I will do that," but I had a plan to outsmart her. I was sure Andres would not be turned on by a pregnant girl (in this I was mostly right), so I returned to the scene of the first crime.

Chapter 8

There have been times in my life when I wished I could have gone through life without the sad times, without feeling lost, without making mistakes,
but now I understand that life just doesn't work that way. I have made many mistakes,
I've experienced really sad times, and sometimes I've been lost.
But I will always pick myself up, dust myself off, and keep on living my life. God shows me that life is worth living. **Based on Dave Hedges**

My mother was neither unduly excited nor negative about this grandchild. She was busy adjusting to the children having been returned to her. This was such a convoluted case by now; the children had left my mother's house for two years and gone to live with Michelle, and now they were returning after my letter. The press and the lawyers and Families and Children did not know what to do. After my recantation, as my mother had planned, all the people on the case began to wonder if my mother's claims were true and if Michelle and I had made it all up. Michelle failed a lie detector test, and some wondered at Michelle's fury in keeping the children. Was it self-motivated?

My own "team," Anita Boch, Mark Schneider, June Shaw, and Shelly Snodgrass all sensed that I had made this recantation because I had to. They continued believing my original story. They were adamant that I had been a victim of abuse, even if I claimed I wasn't. It was heart-breaking because they had been my only friends. They were the only ones who had seemingly cared about me, and now this recantation made it seem that I had turned against them. But I stuck to the story my mother wanted, to keep peace in the house, have the children return, and, most important, to have a place for my baby to be born. From now on, all my decisions would be to protect my own child. I had given up on protecting myself.

With a family system based on lies like the one I was telling, I found that I hated living with my parents, even though I enjoyed seeing all my siblings again. The children seemed happy to be home again and I blamed myself slightly for the previous family upset. In some ways, I told myself there was a type of progress in my recantation. The younger kids had a home that they had desperately wanted to return to. At least I tried to convince myself of that. To fight against my depression about living at home, I got my GED when I was seven months pregnant. Soon I could go to college.

My time came and I gave birth alone in Hialeah Hospital, although my mother came in at the last minute. She discouraged me from breastfeeding, saying that there was a reason they invented formula. She was so intent on this that she wrapped cellophane tightly around my breasts several times until the milk in my breasts dried up. After this, Danielle was formula fed. I felt a great joy with Danielle, a joy I had never known but now shared with this beautiful girl. She and I were instantly close. I knew I would never hurt her as I had been hurt. Yet, the longer I stayed at home, the clearer the truth became to me — this home was not a safe environment and the other kids had to be protected. Andres was Andres. He had already been a devastating threat to two of us girls. Who knew what he would do next.

I decided to find a way to let my mother know that what I had alleged was the truth all along. I needed to tell her that I had lied to help her. I thought that if she saw the truth of the abuse in black and white, she would finally love me and be kinder to Michelle and Nicole. She would give up this vendetta. She would protect my younger siblings. She would do the right thing. We would finally be a healthy family. She just had to believe me about Andres. I got a small tape recorder that I hid in my purse, and then I asked Andres to give me a ride in his truck to the movie theatre where I still worked (Brent had left, thank God). There we were in the pick-up, and I surreptitiously switched on the recorder.

"Did you like having sex with me, Andres?"

"Of course; you were my favorite. You have always had a perfect body. In fact, we should start having sex again, Meme. Not in this car though. Too uncomfortable. I'm talking about a good-time fuck."

"You liked it even when I was twelve, when you devirginized me?"

"Yes, baby, even when you were twelve."

"I know you liked it," I said, "because you always wanted to do it every

49

day."

"Yes," he laughed, "that was a fantastic thing. Me there and you there, and we had some good times, don't you think? I can't wait to fuck you again."

I said, "Well, you know that it hurt a lot, the way you put things inside me and the anal sex."

"Oh no," Andres said, "you just didn't know it, but you liked it. I am sure of it."

I clicked off the machine. "Thanks for the ride, Andres." "Okay, honey. See you later."

I played the same trick on him the next time he gave me a ride and we continued "sharing." On this ride, he mentioned, "I can't wait to do it with you again," among other suggestive pleas. I added that tape to the one I had. I gave the tapes to my mother, I gave the tapes to my team, and I gave the tapes to Michelle; she gave the tapes to the *Miami Herald* writer, Liz Balmaseda, who had been reporting on the case. Ms. Balmaseda's last article on our family described the tapes, stating the man on the tapes sounded exactly like Andres, that they could not possibly have been faked, and called what happened "a tragedy gone wrong," in that the parents had not been charged with their crimes and that the children had been returned. The *New Times* also mentioned the tapes and those tapes were eventually sent to the Governor of Florida. The press and the lawyers wanted to show a mishandling of justice.

Even with the tapes and Andres' voice, my mother still defended her husband. This was perhaps one of the worst parts for me, since even with proof she was saying she didn't care about what had happened to me. I had always been the lost child in the family, but this was the final, irrevocable statement that she preferred to demonize me and stand by her clearly sick husband. I had to face it and the grief was unbearable. If I had not had God's love and Danielle's love, I do not believe I would have survived.

I did not know there is a law against taping conversations without consent and my mother did go public, saying she wanted to prosecute me. But in the end, she did not charge me for recording the tapes because that would make the tapes admissible in court and Andres would face charges. When the case started in 1989, the lawyers were able to suspend Andres' pediatrician license. My tapes were able to keep the license suspended forever, but that was the only outcome from providing proof of his crimes. After five long years, somehow everyone was exhausted and just dropped the ball, but the line had been drawn for me. I had no home with my mother, and now I knew I never would. Danielle, who was then less than one year old, and I moved to Michelle's remodelled home to live in her garage.

My mother did warn me to keep Brent away from Danielle. This was one piece of advice that would come to haunt me. I had not informed him about Danielle's birth, and he did not seem to care. Michelle's husband, Rick, would come out to the garage to visit me and the baby; he was always encouraging me to have a drink with him. I was grateful to have this place to stay, where I was away from my mother. I was deeply wounded that my mother had so clearly shown her support for a man who had admitted on tape to abusing me as a child. It was a constant pain that felt so unfair and like such a black rejection of me; a few drinks were not the worst idea then.

Rick kept visiting the garage, insisting on pouring me more drinks on each visit. On one of these visits, after too many drinks, I passed out (I later learned that I do not have a high alcohol tolerance), and he, like so many before him, raped me. He was another man who must have thought, *she has been through this a lot. What's one more?*

I did not tell Michelle. I did not want to hurt her after her kindness to me. Years later, I was to learn years that Rick was also inappropriate with Nicole, who was staying there, as I was. I would later learn that Rick was a bad guy; he was abusive to Michelle and not always nice to the other kids. It seems Michelle had married (and would soon divorce) our past. When we had been there three months, it was clear once again that I would have to leave. I moved in with a friend and began focusing solely on Danielle. And so began a new battle that I had not foreseen.

Chapter 9

The next time you're stressed, take a step back, inhale, and laugh. Remember who you are and why you're here. You're never given anything in this world that you can't handle.
Be strong, be flexible, love yourself, and love others.
Always remember, just keep moving forward. **Lorenzo Dozier**

"The Case from Hell" had now officially ended, and I began to think about family and how it is important, even if my own family was a disaster. I thought it would be the proper thing to do for Danielle to know her father. I decided she had a right to this, so when she was ten months old I brought my little girl to meet her dad. Perhaps it was pride. I had such a beautiful daughter, despite all that I had been through.

I knew where Brent lived because I had been living there with him when I got pregnant. Brent answered the door, and, happily for me, he was moved by this hazel-eyed, gentle, bouncing baby girl. He oohed and aahed over her, amazed at how special and sweet she was, which she continues to be to do this day, as a grown up. He had read about "The Case from Hell" in the paper and asked me some questions about it. *Was it really true that I had been so abused? Did I really make the tapes? Was my mother really that callous?* He seemed a bit embarrassed about everything that I had been through. He asked about the movie theater and the cast of characters there and we both laughed a bit, but mostly he asked me about Danielle's personality, where we were living, and what my plans were. I answered as best I could, but I was still embarrassed and confused by everything I had been through. I was just living in the moment with my little girl, going day to day, and giving her as much love as I could.

I had forgotten that once a nasty person, always a nasty person. Brent took Danielle from my arms, as would be natural for a father. She began to fuss, and

I reached out for her since it was clear she wanted her mother back. He held her tighter and would not pass her to me, as if she were his possession.

"You have to stay here with me," he said, raising his face and sizing me up, "if you want her back."

"What?" I asked. I looked at him as if he were crazy, but I was not about to get into a physical fight with him, especially with a baby there. I was going to have to outsmart this. He could be violent. "Okay," I said, and I spent the night. I could see that he did not want to let us go. In his way, he was in his kind of love with me, I understood it, but he knew nothing of what it really is to love someone, which is to give. He was a taker, and he wanted my most prized possession. I acted calm, cool, and collected and he left in the morning to go to the awning business he had started after leaving the movie theater. I knew he would leave because everything at the business depended on him. That's when Danielle and I got the hell out of there.

I had no desire to be with him; I had simply thought that a daughter deserves to know her father. I went back to where I was staying. Two months later, I got a notice that Brent was taking me to court seeking full custody of Danielle, claiming parental alienation, which is grounds, it turned out, to take away a child. "Parental alienation" meant that I was turning her against him and keeping him from seeing her. This was a little odd since she was still under a year old. I had been doing the opposite by introducing them to each other. I saw a lawyer who drafted papers stating Brent would have to pay $200 a month for child support. The judge gave him weekend visiting rights, as well as holidays and summer with his daughter. I thought this was a nice compromise for a man who probably would have punched us if I had tried to leave his house. We waited for his response. Two weeks later I received another notice; this one threatened removal of my daughter. Like Brent, his lawyer seemed to lack any compassion.

My lawyer looked at the papers and said, "You're in for a long fight. He's got a list of reasons why you are not a competent mother."

"But I am."

"I know that," the lawyer said, "but on paper it doesn't look like that. You are poor. You have a history of abuse. But don't worry. We will fight it. What are you doing right now in your life?"

"I just enrolled in college. To be a nurse."

"Great," he said. "That shows you are stable… Where do you work?" This was a bit embarrassing, but I was well-aware I had to make decent money to pay a lawyer. I'd had to find ways to make far more than minimum wage, considering that lawyers charge far more than minimum wage.

"You guys cost a lot of money," I said, "not to mention the babysitters I need. I have been stripping at the Solid Gold."

He nodded and I saw he did not write that fact into my dossier. Danielle was making noises and smiling at me intermittently while the lawyer and I were having this conversation. I thought my heart would break. The pain of possibly losing my baby made everything I had endured with Andres and my family look easy. I had already lost all my original family, my home, my credibility, not to mention my innocence, and now I faced losing the only thing I had left in my life, my daughter who had become my world.

Brent had a vengeance, which I had forgotten, but this vengeance was unnatural; something seemed off. I had tried to be civilized by allowing her to see him weekends and have holiday time with him, but when we spoke, he said he would fight me, even if it took forever until he got full custody, and I paid him child support. I was going to learn that these were not casual words. He meant it and he had the means to fight. I did not have the means to fight him back and he knew it. I did, however, have every intention of staying with my daughter, no matter what. If he wanted to embarrass me, harass me, hound me, tell stories about me (and he did), I was not going to let her be taken from me.

We would make it on my earnings and eventually I would have a real job. All I could take comfort in was God and the Virgin Mary. When we got home, I made a pact with God. I put Danielle down for a nap, lit a candle, and told God that He and Mary must fill in now and be the parents that I did not have. He would have to support me in this fight and help me keep Danielle. I promised to talk to Him a lot, to pray daily, and to only shed my tears to Him and to His Blessed Mother. I knew I would keep my promise and thus I did not feel alone. I felt I was and would be carried on unseen wings. Danielle and I would get through this. That bull from my dream now had Brent's face, and Brent had every intention of shattering my house, whatever that took, to take the only person I could trust and had bonded with, the only person who was my flesh and blood whom I could love —he wanted to take her away from me.

Chapter 10

I am in competition with no one. I run my own race. I have no desire to play the game
of being better than anyone, in any way, shape, or form.
I just aim to improve, to be better than I was before, one day at a time.
That's me and I'm free. Have a blessed day. **Jenny Perry**

Brent had now married Candy, an aggressive and self-important woman who used to follow us around when he and I were together. He would say about her, "That girl is obsessed with me." After I left him, Candy was able to forge a relationship with him. I later learned from Danielle that Candy had told him if he married her, he would have a better chance of getting his daughter. There was truth to her words. He and Candy acted like a normal family, especially as they went on to have three children. They looked like the all-American family, the Brady family, except they were far from it in reality. Candy became just as involved as Brent was in fighting me in court for Danielle. In her own way, she was a mastermind of tactics. Perhaps Brent had to focus on work and let her be the instigator. This was all odd because much of Brent's vendetta against me was his obsession with me. What Candy got out from that, I am not sure. I guess if they won in court, it would prove to Brent that I was worthless and she, Candy, was the valuable one; it would be legal proof that she was a better choice than me. Brent, it also turned out, had been and continued to be a difficult man. Danielle said that when she went to visit, he would talk about me compulsively, as if he was still living in the time we were together years ago. Danielle never saw affection between Candy and him. I knew he had beaten the woman before me, Jolyn, and she had taken sole custody of their son, Andrew. He did not pursue this child as he pursued Danielle. This was part of the strangeness of it all. To this day, neither Danielle nor any of her half-sisters have ever met Andrew.

More than anything, Brent wanted to punish me for leaving him, and he used the court system and the threat of taking Danielle away from me as a continual beating. My life became one long custody battle with him. I had to be lawyered up every minute. If I won against him, almost the next day, he was filing against me again. I was incompetent, a bad mother, an evil person… just look at "The Case from Hell," he would argue vehemently. Clearly, I was unstable. I had to listen to this over and over from a variety of lawyers' mouths.

I felt alone in the world, and I was very poor. I knew the decks were stacked against me unfairly. They had a big family, they were much richer, and they had an aggressive, dishonest attorney. I would get severely depressed and just want to stay in bed and hide, but I knew I had to stay in college to prove to the judge that I was not the broken mother they portrayed me to be. I managed to attend my classes toward a nursing psychology degree at Miami Dade, even though sometimes it felt like I could not even lift the blankets off myself in bed. I had very good reasons to want to stay in bed. I was spending all too many of my days in court with Brent, who walked in with documented, stamped fabrications. I would break down in tears, begging the judge to believe that these court dates were frivolous proceedings. "Brent does see his daughter every other weekend and I am complying," I would say, and I did honor that agreement because I was fearful of being taken to court. How ironic since I was being taken to court anyway.

"You think I want to go through this?" I would say to the judge. "What can I do to prove the truth?" I was always on the losing end and the judge probably didn't change custody because I looked so pathetic. Stripping at night undoubtedly did not help my case, so I only did it for six months. I knew the money was better than a normal waitressing job, and I needed good money to be able to afford the lawyers, and the truth was that I did not like doing this work. Although I like dancing and I love music, having to deal with men leering at me was an unhealthy environment for me. There is no doubt that those hungry, surreptitious looks might have had something to do with the intensity of my depression at that time. They subconsciously jolted me into my past. I danced, but I kept my distance.

The stripping was getting to me, so I decided to go work at Hooters™. There I met my best friend Jennifer, with whom I would have a twenty-five-year friendship. She is a buxom blonde from Massachusetts, with pretty girl-next-door looks and a sharp tongue. When I met her, she felt like a kind of "big sister" to me. I remember one time we were in a car with some other girls from the bar who were being hard on me and trying to start a fight. Jennifer turned around and said, "Don't you ever touch a mother with her child." She took me under her wing.

Part of that wing involved doing cocaine after work at the bar. It was not ideal for a young mother, but this young mother was working all the time to make enough money to fight Brent while raising her daughter. This young mother had to pay the costs of attending Miami Dade College. This young mother felt under constant attack by the threat of possibly losing the one thing she cared about: Danielle. The cocaine provided a relief from hearing in court that I was a slut, a bad mother, and every other lie in the book. I thought it was only a matter of time before certain judges would fall for Brent and his very adept lawyer's tricks. Fortunately, he did not have much to use against me, so he never won. I began to see that his strategy was simply to tire me out, breaking me down financially and emotionally.

This was not a good strategy, given that I adored my sweet little daughter as she was growing. She had become my best friend. We were inseparable. We had much light, laughter, and caring in our relationship. I'd experienced something so much darker with my mother's bad mothering that I was never going that way. But the attorneys that I was continually having to hire were expensive and working at Hooters™ didn't even pay their retainer, never mind their entire fee. They say a mother will cut off her right arm for her child. Jennifer suggested that I do a short stint in Chicago on weekends as a high-end escort. She would come with me as moral support. We could drink there afterward, use cocaine to get me through it, and I would make $5,000 a night.

Five thousand dollars was exactly the kind of money I needed. My legal and court fees were exorbitant and every time I made a simple phone call, I'd rack up a $250 bill, which was one week's pay. Public defenders could not take me on as a client because the case had already started. It seemed Brent always had another ace up his sleeve whenever we went to court. He and his attorney would come with their stories: I didn't deliver Danielle to him when I said I would, I left her alone all the time. They came with these accusations written down in well-organized file folders. I would stand quietly next to my lawyer and listen to these lies and want to jump over the aisle and wring his neck. But I just stood there and had to listen to more.

"She does not answer her phone when the father calls about seeing his daughter." A lie.

"My client never sees his daughter." Another lie.

"She is poisoning his daughter against him." Another lie.

"She takes drugs with her daughter there." Another lie. I only did cocaine with Jennifer when Danielle wasn't around.

Brent refused to relent. Two of my attorneys quit, overwhelmed by how ruthless he and his lawyer were. I needed a killer attorney to equal his. I found one, George Vogelsang, but he charged $1000 a day. I didn't hesitate to hire him, because I never hesitated in my quest to keep my daughter. That is why I felt I had to do whatever it took.

Off Jennifer and I went to Chicago to a fancy hotel. I was given a room number and there would be a man, usually married, waiting. Danielle would be visiting her father or on holidays. I would do my work, and afterward, Jennifer and I would go to the bar to relax. It was interesting that as close as we were, I never told her about my past. I kept it quiet. She probably knew that I had been abused, but I felt that this was my pain to bear alone. These weekly trips allowed me to pay my attorney, but this work was not easy. Sometimes I felt that I was being raped. Certain men felt that paying an escort meant they could take out all their aggression on me. They would tear off my clothes, call me names, and try to hurt me. Not all the men were like this. I got through it by convincing myself this was merely a transaction; I justified it by believing the client and I were just helping each other. The client was lonely or angry or maybe his wife refused to have sex, and I needed the money to keep my daughter. I remember one client who was a good person and who said, "I really appreciate my time with you because I know you will not be in this racket long." He was right. This "job," like the stripping, was compounding my depression. I could not respect myself. I was so sad during this time of my life that I went to church every morning and cried to God. I begged Him to take this whole pain of court and financial stress away from me.

I must say that I chose to do this "work" rather than live with my sister Michelle because I didn't want to be a burden to her. She already had a large family, and it was my priority not to be what I thought was a bother. Each one of us had tremendous problems and I wanted to make my own way. I didn't trust interactions with my family; even if I had to do anything to make ends meet, I did not want to get involved with all the bad-mouthing. Sometimes I thought Brent's vehemence came from the fact he was jealous of me. I remembered that when we were together, we both considered getting our GEDs at the same time. We each took the free test, but it turned out he needed classes before he could take his test, and I didn't. With all I had been through, I think Brent thought I had an easier pass than him. Of course, this was distorted thinking, but distorted thinking was one of his fortes.

Spending time in court was bad enough, but there was another sadness that Brent was bringing upon me and my daughter. When Danielle was supposed to see him, I had to force my toddler to see him; otherwise, Brent would have something on me in court. She would cry, beg, cling to me, and refuse to go. A child knows exactly what is going on, and even though Brent and Candy might seemingly have had a more normal living situation, Danielle intuitively knew that her father's interest in her was not about her. It didn't matter how much I tried to convince Danielle that her dad loved and missed her, that she had a big fun family with him, she always dreaded staying there. She knew it was more about revenge for him. With me, she got love.

I could see that Danielle was beginning to suffer from emotional and psychological abuse since Brent was using her as a pawn. She was extraordinarily shy and reluctant to speak. She was clingy and nervous. I decided the only thing I could do to safeguard Danielle would be to take her to counseling on a weekly basis as soon as she was able to talk. (Another cost!) There was one pleasant surprise at this time; even amid escorting and working, even while mothering and fighting with Brent, I found I was enjoying my classes at college. I somehow managed to always be on the honor roll.

Around this time, a hurricane hit Cape Florida, and as a part of our environmental studies curriculum, the university students were sent down to help rebuild the area. I found that working in the dirt and nature, tearing down dead trees was therapeutic. Whatever class I was in, I seemed to excel. Even so, I still went through horrible bouts of physical pain, my depression manifesting somatically. I would sleep too much, or not want to take baths, or just stay in the dark in my house. I was living on a wing and a prayer, holding my breath; I would be lying if I did not admit that Brent's relentlessness and tactics were starting to make me lose hope. Even so, there were some signs that we might get through this. And, as the Bible says, one of those signs was to come from the mouth of babes.

Chapter 11

Part 1 of the Peace Prayer of Saint Francis:

Lord, make me an instrument of your peace:
Where there is hatred, let me sow love;
Where there is injury, pardon:
Where there is doubt, faith;
Where there is despair, hope;
Where there is darkness, light;
Where there is sadness, joy.

By the time Danielle was three years old, so many things had gone wrong that I started to lose my faith. I began turning to cocaine more often to self-medicate my fear and loneliness. I began to think God chose not to answer prayers if He designated you to suffer. Danielle was slow in starting to talk, but one morning I went into her room. She was lying on her stomach, and as she was waking up, she said, "Mom, God was looking at me while I was sleeping." It was so good to hear her speak. I sat down on the bed and stroked her hair. "Did you see Him?"

"No, He was behind me, looking down. I was sleeping."

Then I realized she wasn't making it up. No one ever sees the face of God. "Did He say anything?"

"He said, 'Come back to me, my child.'"

This brought tears to my eyes because that was exactly what He had said to me when I had my own dream at seven years old: "Come to me, my child." I was in awe, goosebumps all over my limbs. I was receiving a message through her. God was speaking to me again and He still loved me. He did understand how it was killing me to face losing my daughter at least three times a year to a family who seemed to enjoy inflicting pain. I wanted better for my daughter. God was reminding me through Danielle that He was still there.

"That sounds like a magnificent dream," I said, as I helped her dress.

Once I had given her breakfast, I went to the Virgin Mary statue I kept in my house, and as Danielle played around me, I prayed now harder than ever. I got some marvelous answers. One of them was, of all things, to let myself fall madly in love with a man who had been chasing me and who could provide some stability for Danielle and me, a man who knew me and my story completely. This man was the German lawyer, Mark Schneider, who had been on my "team" when I was fifteen, while I was going through all the troubles with "The Case from Hell."

I would see him as I went in and out of the courthouse for my hearings with Brent. Mark would be there for his own cases. We'd run into each other and, of course, now I was no longer a teenager. I was twenty-three years old. He'd see me going in for the battle and give me a thumbs up. Sometimes he'd yell out, "Aimee, you'll win this," or, "Have you thought about taking up law since you're always here anyway?" He was very handsome, tall, well dressed, sure of himself, and accomplished. I could see that he took delight in seeing me and I was complimented. It was only a matter of time before he asked me out for dinner and he said the magic words, "Aimee, after everything I saw you go through, I am so struck by how you have remained an amazing person." We went to fashionable places, and he made me feel beautiful. I think he truly admired my grit. He could see how I was struggling, and I appreciated that he took the trouble to take in the reality of my life. When we began dating more and more, he got to know Danielle and he was kind to her and, of course, this warmed my heart even more.

After some time had passed, he said, "Aimee, it would be better for you if you moved in with me in my condo in Brickell. You can focus on your studies then and not worry so much about expenses." And this was the first answer to my prayer.

I was now with a man I loved, and I no longer had bills to worry about. I was extremely grateful for both. I could finally go to school fulltime. I had a red, beat-up Renault which broke down all the time, but thankfully it was a short distance to go back and forth to classes. The ability to accelerate my education meant that I could soon go to the University of Miami. Mark had a Ferrari, an airplane, a house in Key West, and a beautiful condo, so all of this was a complete change from the way I had been living. I loved his intelligence and his thinking, and we were compatible on a day-to-day basis. However, he had certain rigidities. He would never give me any money or help with my custody battles. I considered that of little importance, compared to everything else he was giving. I was happy.

The other answered prayer was a little more circuitous. The judge handed my never-ending custody case to the General Master Melissa Tennenbaum. I think the judge was exhausted by the continual drama of these two parents showing up with the same battle cries and defenses that seemed only to be circular. Maybe he thought a new mind would be able to bring fresh solutions to the case. Unfortunately, Ms. Tennenbaum read all the documentation against me and took Brent and Candy's version as the truth. She didn't seem to pay much attention to my story, especially when my documentation, if any, was sparse, and the fact that I had moved so often appeared to indicate my instability. It was the three of them against me. I didn't have a lawyer since I had stopped escorting and working, partially due to being with Mark and partially because when I did work, moments of depression would inhibit my performance.

There I was in court, standing alone. and pleading with her, but she was not interested. She looked over her glasses at me and said, "You are not capable." She was referring to me as a mother. Brent and his lawyer smiled at each other and shook hands as if they had won the Nobel Prize. I felt sick to my stomach.

"We will convene at the next hearing and custody will be finalized," she continued. "Court dismissed." I went home appalled. I could not even look at Brent or his lawyer when I walked out. Later, I sat in Mark's living room thinking. One advantage of living with a lawyer is you become a bit of a lawyer yourself, or at least I did. I was always hearing about this statute and that motion and this argument. I could sense that unless I did something, I would lose my daughter in the next hearing. Ms. Tennenbaum had already made up her mind. I could see it. I picked up one of the motions against me and went to the legal library. I began researching statutes to see what I could do, and I realized that my only option was to recuse this General Master based on prejudice and bias, something that my last attorney had refused to do; he had quit, instead.

I ran into a young attorney at the library who was curious about what a young woman was so intently researching. I briefly explained what I was doing. "I want to make a motion showing that Melissa Tennenbaum is being prejudicial. She is not interested in hearing my side of the case. She has already made up her opinion based on false evidence, their documented lies."

"I know exactly what statutes you need," he said kindly, referring me to the exact literature that could help me. I typed a motion using the same language and format that lawyers used to write their motions. It looked exactly like an attorney's motion. Interestingly, when my motion was to be petitioned, it was to her, of all people. She read it and then looked up, and this time, over her glasses, she said, "Motion granted on the basis of my bias." She must have realized that she was wrong and the fact that the hearings were recorded would possibly come back against her. She had no choice but to recuse herself from the case. I was so proud of myself! It proved to me that we can always take actions for ourselves. It was a major victory. The next time we were all in court, the older original male judge —Judge Gross was back. He looked out at us despondently. I could see him thinking, *them again.*

"This case," he said, "is getting nowhere and I have no desire to hear it twenty more times. I will appoint a psychiatrist that you will both agree to be an expert witness to determine custody. I will make my decision based solely on this. I no longer know whom to believe in testimony."

Brent's attorney suggested Dr. Lopez-Brignoni and I agreed. Brent and Candy saw her first. Then it was my turn to go with Danielle. Dr. Lopez-Brignoni was a prominent psychiatrist, a heavy-set Spanish woman, rather like my mother, but she seemed to understand and believe my story. She asked me many questions and she was thorough in questioning me about mothering. She did not reveal her feelings. She interviewed Danielle. I knew my living situation was more tenuous than Brent's, even though I was now living with Mark. We were not married. I knew that I did not make money at that point. I knew that I had a past. I did not know what she would do.

The day came for the final judgment. It seemed this would be "it." It was a hot day. The air conditioning was not working. I was not sure whether that fact alone would bode badly for me. The judge asked, "Dr. Lopez-Brignoni, with whom do you recommend that the child live?" She answered from the witness chair, looking professional in her blue suit, "Your Honor, there is structure with the father but nurture with the mother."

The judge looked a bit surprised by her succinctness, but he was probably grateful. He said, "Thank you, Doctor, but, in your estimation, which is more important?"

We all waited for her answer as if it was a murder verdict and, in a way, it was.

"A child needs nurture," she said. I felt my heart jump in relief, knowing that God must really love me. I couldn't stay still since I felt like I had been holding my breath the last few years. It was as if I had been living in war-time and now they had called an armistice. The judge turned to me, "Your daughter, Ms. Cabo, can stay with you. I ask you, Mr. Brent Jones, and Mrs. Candice Jones, to let the mother and daughter live in some peace. Ms. Cabo does let you see your daughter, so for now, I do not want to see this case in my court again. Court dismissed." We had a reprieve.

That night I thanked God again and then Danielle, Mark, Jennifer, and I had a party, celebrating with hugs, candles, and cake. Mark said, "I wonder if I should hire Aimee as an assistant to work on my cases."

Jennifer said, "I'll negotiate her rates."

Mark laughed and I even had the pleasure of seeing Danielle join in, smiling and talking a little bit to Mark. That night was a happy one, but I knew there would only be a short recess from the custody battle. Brent was not the type to ever let me win.

Chapter 12

Part Two of the Peace Prayer of Saint Francis

O divine Master,
grant that I may not so much seek
To be consoled as to console,
To be understood as to understand,
To be loved as to love.
For it is in giving that we receive,
It is in pardoning that we are pardoned,
And it is in dying that we are born to eternal life.
Amen.

I decided to start occasional therapy with Dr. Lopez-Brignoni because there was no question that even though I was with Mark and we were getting a reprieve with the custody battles, I was still battling severe depression. Danielle started seeing her on a weekly basis as well. I forced myself to be cheerful with people so I would not be a burden to them, but when Mark was at work and I was not in classes, I felt as if I was being chased by something horrible inside and outside of me that was going to destroy me. I wanted to hide, and I would take any drug I could get my hands on to calm my anxiety when I felt afraid and vulnerable. I couldn't stand the feeling of panic that took over me.

Dr. L-B (as I'll refer to her) prescribed medication for depression and this medication allowed me to stop self-medicating with drugs, but often the medication would not work. I would find myself staying in bed all day, hoping I could sleep the whole time. I would only get up to use the bathroom or make Danielle something to eat. At one point, my depression was so bad that I remember having Danielle bring me the gallon of milk and cereal to my bed and that's where I would prepare her breakfast. Mark would be gone at the crack of dawn and home late, working on his cases. I was riddled with nightmares and nervous about doing normal daily activities. I barely ate and I was down to 105 pounds, for my five- foot-one-inch frame.

When the depression hit, I would believe that I hadn't been meant to be born, that somehow, I deserved everything I'd suffered. Much of this was caused by what Brent would drag up in court. He had become friendly with my mother, which was bad enough, and he would say in court, "Even her mother agrees that she is a liar, unstable, and not worthy of raising her child." Then he would go on, claiming parental alienation. This was like having a knife stuck in me. And he loved repeating it. Brent had made himself my enemy and his main ammunition was bringing my mother in as if they were a united army against me. It was hard for me to live with the fact that my own mother had not sided with me after hearing the tapes that validated her husband's abuse of me. I could not get over that she chose to side with a man who wanted to hurt me and my daughter, a man who liked spending all his money telling the world how horrible I was. I would lie in bed and think, *what kind of person are you, Aimee, to have a child with such a vindictive person?* All of it was torture. The only time my prescribed medication seemed to work was when I prayed daily, and I knew my strength came from God.

I had never liked therapy, but I kept seeing Dr. L-B anyway, and I found I liked her. We could speak Spanish and I admired her strength and her mind, which reminded me of the good traits of my mother. I looked at my sessions with Dr. L-B as having a conversation with a friend who gives sound advice, but most of all, she was a good listener, and she didn't push me by filling the silence with irrelevant conversation. She was not like the roster of constantly changing psychiatrists I'd had in the hospital who would only ask one question: How are you feeling? Then, they would prescribe medication that either didn't work or made me even more depressed.

At that time, I didn't talk to my friends or even to Mark about all the troubles in my life; I wanted to be nothing but happy and fun for them so they would not abandon me too. I didn't have to rehash my past with Dr. L-B because she already knew me from "The Case from Hell" days. She was down to earth about it and seemed to care. The medications she prescribed started to work, so I started to see her only every six weeks to refill my medication until I developed a resistance and needed a new medication. But Brent and Candy started up again, using "parental alienation" once more as their argument. Back we were, with me having to listen to Brent's and his lawyer's distorting stories. Even worse was hearing what he was doing to Danielle.

"Dad keeps talking about you." "What does he say?" I asked.

"That you don't know how to be a mother."

I put my head down and said, "I am sorry, honey. You know I love you."

And then this little girl smiled and said, "I told him you make dinner for me every day." We both hugged. Of course, if Mark was away, I mostly took her out for fast food, which was cheaper in some ways, but she was trying to protect me from Brent as well. It broke my heart she would even have to do this.

"What did he say?"

"He says he will take me away from you." Then she started to cry, adding, "Don't let him."

"I won't, honey. You know that." I assured her, but I wasn't sure how long I could fight him. He never gave up. I wanted to continue taking Danielle to therapy with Dr. L-B, but now Brent and Candy began opposing this with a vengeance. They hated Dr. L-B because she had thrown out their last case against me. I found a new psychiatrist for Danielle, and my daughter also began making progress. For both of us, the process was slow, but we were dedicated. Mark was steady with me, and it seemed like things were moving forward, with just the occasional bad days. Maybe I had lulled that bull to sleep a little bit.

Chapter 13

Lord, like David, I need your encouragement in a time of trial and anguish.
Thank You that You are always on the throne, always my God, ready to save.
Thank You for being the same God to me that you were to David.
Thank You for always being near and always rescuing me from my fears
and hurts.
Lord, help me remember that daybreak might just be ahead, that this trial
will not last forever.
Fill me with the hope that daybreak is coming and that Your love will
always prevail!
In Jesus' name, amen! **Unknown author**

After my second trip to the Dominican Republic when I had become engaged to Bobby, I had kept in touch with my sister Nicole. I was now planning my wedding with Bobby; he and I had decided to have our wedding on Christmas Day, a month from when he proposed, since we considered each other to be a gift. Nicole was to be my maid of honor; after all, she had been there when Bobby and I first met. It was fitting.

I was poor then, since I had long left Mark, the lawyer, so I decided to wear a simple, pretty, white summer dress that I already owned. I couldn't even afford dental care at that time. I was only chewing on one side of my mouth since I was missing a molar. But sisters are sisters, no matter what terrible childhood events have happened. Nicole told Michelle about my upcoming wedding, and a week before I left for my wedding, Michelle, ever the older sister, showed up at my door with a beautiful simple wedding dress, just right for the ceremony we had planned on the beach, followed by a reception in a garden. Michelle couldn't come to the wedding but agreed to help me be a sponsor for Bobby when I petitioned for him to come to the US where we would live as husband and wife.

Danielle could not come to the wedding either; at seven years old, it would require a legal proceeding for her to leave the country and we all knew how that would go. She would meet her stepdad when the time came. Wonderfully, Bobby's parents, who are kind and good people like Bobby, came from Bulgaria to witness their oldest son get married. It was a beautiful day. There were flowers everywhere, and I felt as if I was in a dream in this lovely dress, marrying this even lovelier man. We married in front of a judge, and as anyone who has married that way knows, that kind of wedding is so brief, you hardly know it happened. You say, "I do," and it's over. It's almost funny that this huge event in our lives happened at the speed of light, but it meant everything to both of us in the long-term. Anyway, it was to be the first of three weddings for Bobby and me, and I mean three weddings that we had with each other! That's not to say that we didn't party it up. I threw Bobby into the pool fully dressed and then Nicole threw me in, still wearing my wedding dress. We spent two weeks in the honeymoon villa, where we arrived the first night to see two towels on our bed that were folded like swans into the shape of a heart. Swans stay faithful for life and never leave their mates. It was exactly right.

It was the second happiest day of my life, the first being the birth of Danielle. I looked at it as the end of a nightmare, although it was not the end, by any means, of our troubles. We were still in for some very heavy blows from that bull, perhaps the heaviest yet, but for those two weeks, we were ecstatic. Never for a minute, even with the suddenness of this marriage, did we think we might have made a mistake. It proved to me there is such a thing as a soulmate. Bobby was the first man to whom I could tell anything, the first man who stood up for me, who went through life fully with me. He was the first man who knew how to care for me and the first man who was not only brilliant and ambitious, but also kind. For that entire two weeks, I bathed in God's love for me and I was grateful.

But two weeks came to an end, and for a year and a half we had to go our separate ways and keep seeing each other in the way we had before until his papers came through. This was a minor inconvenience compared to the promise of a full and beautiful life with this man I loved.

I went home, glowing, to my other love, Danielle. I showed her pictures and what little girl does not love a fairy tale complete with a fairy tale dress? What little girl does not like her mother being the princess? It tells her that she, too, will be a princess one day, like her mother. We sat on the couch together and I told her she was going to love her stepdad. She was going to have security. There would be no fighting around her so she would have a real feeling of wholeness. Then she asked me the oddest question, "How have you been able to keep me all these years? I know my dad and Candy are always fighting you." I was struck again by how kids don't miss a trick.

She added, "You don't seem as worried anymore. Is it because of my new dad?"

I decided the best way to handle questions was to tell the truth. We all know it had got me in trouble in life, but it had also freed me. I would do it again. I snuggled up to her and said, "Yes, your father has been very difficult for me to deal with, but then a magical thing happened."

"What?" she asked, her dark eyes dancing. "What magical thing? Bobby?"

"Yes, that is one, but there was something else, and it shows God is on our side. One day, I met a young lawyer when I was out with Jennifer, and he had a big heart. I told him about my troubles with all these custody cases. I thought he could give me advice, but, instead, he took my case, for free. He was no match for your father's attorney, who is very strong and does whatever he wants to do to win. Anyway, the young lawyer went off to a new firm and then God blessed us." "How?" she said, although I suspect maybe her eyes were a bit glazing over with all this legal business. Whose wouldn't?

"Well," I continued (I think she would have listened rapturously to me reciting phone books since she was still in the dream of seeing her mother as a princess, not to mention her mother was still in the dream of being a princess), "that lawyer's boss, Jay Levy, took our case, and he is very honest, but…"

She looked up. "…he is the smartest fighter I ever saw." "Like a superhero?" she asked.

"Exactly. When your dad's lawyer went for Mr. Levy, Mr. Levy fought back brilliantly. Your dad's attorney finally met his match. Mr. Levy is still working for us, and he never charges us. He has never charged us all this time. He is a special, good man, and maybe he prepared me to trust in Bobby."

"What is he like?" Danielle asked, a little bit fascinated by this savior.

"You'll meet Bobby and love him. You saw how handsome and smart he is in the pictures."

"I know," she said, "but I meant the fighting lawyer…"

"Oh, Jay. He was moved by my being a single mother with such a beautiful daughter," I said, stroking her hair. "He is straightforward and super smart. He is a trial lawyer. When Bobby and I get on our feet, we're going to pay him, since the battle is sure to go on. You know that."

Danielle smiled. "I know. Did you want to marry the lawyer?"

I laughed. "No, honey, he is married, and I was meant by God for Bobby. But Jay Levy is important to us. Every lawyer quit on me," I said, "because it was so hard dealing with your father's lawyer, but Jay Levy stayed with us. He never sued the other lawyer for the terrible things he said, he just defends us brilliantly." Danielle said, "Wow," although I doubted she understood what I was saying.

"And now," I said, tucking her in, "God has brought you a new father who is the most wonderful person. And we have Jay, too, helping us. God's love is changing our lives for the better."

"Better than when you were with Mark, right?" she asked.

How do these kids know so much? I wondered.

"Yes, better than when we were with Mark."

I kissed her and then I went to my room and lay down, happy, so happy, about Bobby and me. I thought it was interesting that I was talking about Jay the same night I was talking about my wedding. I wondered why, but then I realized it was because Jay Levy had the kind of values I admired and so, it seemed, did Bobby.

I was not ever to be wrong in either of those assessments. I turned over in bed and could not get over my blessings. I realized how remarkable it was that I had gotten here.

Chapter 14

Lord, I am weary, and I don't know when this "race" will end in my life. I feel like I've been running forever, trying to outrun this trial.
Help me to stop trying to outrun my pain but rather run the race You have set before me with endurance. I know that because of You I am ultimately victorious over the trials in my life.
I know that nothing in this world can separate me from Your steadfast love.
Please give me a measure of Your love today; give me the strength to endure this trial.
Thank you for Your love for me that neverends!
And thank you for the crown of joy that awaits me forever in Your Kingdom!
Adrian Rogers

I lived with Mark from the time Danielle was three until she turned six, but things weren't always so easy with Mark. As much as I looked up to him, he could be cruel. He'd go off to Key West parties in his plane and refuse to bring me along. He acted as if he were a god, and I had to put up with anything he did.

When I'd say, "What did you do in Key West?" or something like that, he would reply, "I don't have to tell you what I am doing."

He was rejecting me, and it hit a very wounded nerve, given how I had been rejected by my family. He would not listen to me; he'd go wherever he wanted, and he'd only be nice if he wanted something from me. Otherwise, my life had to revolve around keeping him happy, not asking any questions, and putting up with suspicious behavior.

He could also be verbally abusive, yet we could be passionate at times and I felt my whole life was him. I admired his success and intelligence and so I made myself be willing to do anything or put up with anything to make this work. Sometimes he could be very sweet so it would give me hope that things between us would work out in the end. It was a roller coaster, as these kinds of relationships can be, and my heart would break when he inexplicably turned on me.

But after quite a few years, when Danielle was about six, our relationship looked like it wasn't going to make it. We fought all the time. I was starting to lose my faith in God again, and I could not feel positive footing anywhere. As Mark and I struggled with each other, I lost more and more confidence and I felt my life was only about suffering. What was the point? Nothing ever worked out. I began to think that I was not just the child in the infamous "Case from Hell," I was the adult destined to live in a case from hell. Maybe the other hell, down below, would just be another painful place I could get used to. Maybe I should just end everything, not being loved, being rejected and treated as worthless as I had been by my mother and now by Mark. Maybe it was time to leave this earth.

That is how I ended up swallowing a bottle of aspirin and then brand-new bottle of sleeping pills. I immediately changed my mind. I couldn't do this to Danielle. I couldn't put her through so much pain. I managed to call Mark and told him what I'd done. *Maybe now he will be nice to me*, I thought. *Maybe he will now understand how hard this fighting is for me and he'll be loving.*

By the time he got to me, I could barely walk, and I was extremely sleepy. He could see that I was in a dangerous place, and he rushed me to the hospital emergency room. Right away, they processed me and gave me a bed. I was woozy and hurting and, as I forced my eyes to open to thank Mark, I saw him turning around and leaving. Not even a goodbye, no tender words of encouragement, and no interest in why I might feel this badly. He just ran out of there. I was too sleepy to say anything, but tears ran down my face at his lack of caring. I could see he didn't love me.

They thrust a plastic tube down my throat to my stomach and pumped it without any anaesthesia, maybe to prove to me this is not an easy ordeal to go through. I felt frightened, alone, and very sad when I came to, and I was very aware that Mark was not there. They kept me in the hospital for a couple of days and I only heard from him at the end of those days. I went back to his place, and we tried to resume living together, but then I found out I was pregnant with Mark's child. I was in love with Mark, even though he was a controlling man and not a particularly giving man, and I decided, no matter what, I was going to make this work. We would be a family. He came home from work, and I had fixed him a great dinner and excitedly told him the news. He listened quietly. I was smiling. Then he stood up.

"You are going to have to abort."

What? I thought.

"At least think about it," I said. "It will be a beautiful child."

He didn't answer. How was I going to convince him? This discussion went on every night. I did not believe in abortion, and I also felt we would be happy as a family. He was good with Danielle, and he would love this new child. *He is just scared*, I told myself. That's what I kept believing, but Mark was becoming colder and nastier to me by the day. He found continual fault with me, with how I kept the house (and I am a fastidious cleaner), how I talked, how I thought.

One day, he said, "I want to talk to you."

Good, I thought, *he's coming around.* "I want you and Danielle to move out." "Where?"

"I don't care. I don't want this baby and I don't want to discuss it anymore and you and Danielle are no longer my problem." I felt panicky. Everything was dropping away. We had been arguing about this for four months. I said, "I don't know where to go and I don't have any money." I was terrified that Danielle and I would be homeless. It had always been a fear of mine since I had often been very close to it as a young girl. I could handle many difficulties, but I knew I could not take that. I had a receptionist job, but it would not be enough money to keep us and a new baby together.

"I found a room in a house with a Brazilian woman I know," he said. "I have rented it for you for now." He looked at me, steely- eyed. "It is not negotiable, Aimee, you are going there."

My new landlady was tall and skinny with a strong accent. I looked at it as temporary until Mark came to his senses. I was still trying to complete my studies, but being heartbroken and scared about what to do, I lost my receptionist job. I just cried too much. I went to a Catholic church and three nuns agreed to speak with me. Maybe they will know the answer to this problem. I explained I was four months pregnant, and I needed help. They looked at me.

"We are sorry for your situation," one said. "Do you know the story of Job in the Bible?"

"Kind of," I said.

"Well, he was tested in every way, he lost his money, his family, his health, his property but he never lost faith, and in the end, he was greatly blessed."

One nun stood up and said, "May that happen to you." And that was the help I got.

Okay, I thought, *I will keep my faith,* which had returned to me once I recovered from the pointless pill-taking. My faith wasn't in question for me anyway. What was in question was what to do. Sometimes, doing nothing gives you the answer. I thought that now, at four-and-a-half months pregnant, it was too late to abort. *Maybe Mark will see that and miss me.*

Finally, Mark called me. "I want to see you."

Great, I thought.

"Come over. I have something to show you."

What could it be? A ring? I was so glad to be going home again. When you love someone, or when you think you love someone, you want to be with them. I went to his apartment and there he was in his expensive white shirt and slacks and his perfect haircut, but his mouth was tight.

"Look at this," he said.

He handed me some papers that I unfolded, and there I saw a motion that shocked me. He had petitioned for the removal of custody the minute the child was born. This was a very calculated move on his part, perhaps to be expected from a trial lawyer. He knew my case and my past, and he knew how I had fought for Danielle. He also knew a broken girl, without money or a family, who might be able to consistently fight one mean lawyer for Danielle, but could I fight two lawyers at the same time for each of my children? He knew I didn't have the strength or the resources. I looked at him and the look in his eyes had the same expression of that bull in my dream when it was intent on blowing down my house.

My answer was, "You know I don't believe in abortion. I will carry this child only to give it away and maybe never see her or him again." I thought that might scare him. I had no intention of doing it. Danielle was sitting next to me stroking my hand. She could see the pain I was in, and she was scared. She was stroking my hand because she wanted me to stroke her hand. I looked down at her next to me on the couch and thought, *I can choose this child I have grown to adore or the child not yet born.* I would not win both cases in court. One case had been more than hard enough and all the terrible things I heard about me had put me in a depression from which I was only slowly recovering. I was headed towards losing both children.

Mark could see me thinking. He knew he was probably going to win, something lawyers are trained to do. "Aimee," he said, "I will find you another place to stay and give you money to eat if you abort. It's the only way you can keep Danielle and give her a home. Brent will win by taking her away when he sees how well I do at taking away the other one."

I left there broken-hearted at his lack of love for me, for Danielle, and for our unborn child. The next day, I asked Jennifer to take care of Danielle. That day Mark picked me up and took me to an abortion clinic, and there, dying inside myself, I aborted my unborn child to help the one who was already with me. It haunts me to this day.

I could never imagine Bobby acting that way. He is a doctor who helps people. Mark was a man who knew how to legally destroy people. Mark then began texting me, saying he was in love with me. Of course, he did; I had only ever done what he wanted and had only been good to him. Of course, he loved me. That was love to him. Domination. A year later when I told him I was marrying Bobby, he said, "Don't do it. I now live in Key West. You can come to be with me. You were the right person for me."

Now, the night after I had put Danielle to bed and we'd had our fairy tale talk, I turned over in my bed and picked up the picture I had of Bobby's and my wedding. *Maybe I was the right person for you, Mark,* I thought as I turned off the light, *but you were not the right person for me.*

Chapter 15

Dear Lord,
Thank You for all Your blessings, For my family, friends, and neighbors.
Thank You for all the beauty
In the skies, the lakes, and the mountains.
Thank You for all the excitement of celebration, Birthdays, weddings, and
christenings,
Thank You for all the variety of animals, birds, and insects. Thank You for all the
enrichment of music, art, and literature.
Thank You for the amazing jigsaw puzzle of life!
What a beautiful picture is made when I place all these pieces together!
Thank You for the promise of eternity,
For the sacrifices You made so that I can be free, Free to make my life into a glorious
patchwork of thanksgiving
That carries me onwards to the promises of new heavenly pieces to add to all that I
already hold.
Thank You. Amen. **Unknown**

After Mark and I were finished, sometimes Danielle and I lived alone, sometimes with roommates, or sometimes with a boyfriend. One of the places where I lived was a beautiful small apartment in Kendall. I seemed to have enough money to rent this little place for just the two of us. The realtor, a young man who seemed to have all the time in the world, was very friendly and surprised me a bit when, as he showed me the apartment, he said, "Come in the bathroom here. I have something you will really like."

"What?" I thought it was some unusual detailing in the decor. When I went in there, he had a pipe.

"Try it," he said. "What is it?" "Crack."

I had never smoked crack, but this was a time in my life when all I wanted to do was get away from myself, so I tried it. I was constantly on the lookout for a magical, no frills, no fuss way to escape my constant inner longing for and hurt about Mark, the lost baby, the past, the court battles, all of it. I carried that body of pain with me wherever I went, and it dragged me down. It made it harder for me to move, to think, to envision the future. Danielle was on a visit to her father, *so why not?* I thought.

The crack turned out to be a manic speed train out of myself. It takes you out of your body so quickly, transporting you to another world where everything that burdens you disappears. I couldn't believe it. Fortunately, I did not get hooked on it. Something in me knew: a) I could not afford it, and b) it was too powerful. If I kept taking it, I would lose any sanity or stability, so it never became my drug of choice. I also had the good luck to never try heroin. My attitude about drugs was to do them when they were passed to me by friends or guys and only during my off weekends without Danielle, but I tended not to buy them myself.

This all made sense because my weekends alone were when all my demons came to the fore. One reason was that they always started with Brent finding a way to humiliate me in front of my daughter. Brent lived in Fort Lauderdale, and he refused to drive to Miami to pick her up. I would drive to him in my beat-up car, but that wasn't what bothered me. Danielle and I could sing in the car, and I could prepare her a little bit for what she was about to go through. What was humiliating was that he insisted that the transfer take place in a police station. His reasons, he told the court, were that I might act out, that he needed protection from me, and that I was dangerous. When it came to my daughter, nothing could be further from the truth.

Besides that, Danielle would scream and cry and not want to go; she would beg me not to have to see her father. She would reference Cinderella, since her stepsiblings were favored, and she did not feel welcome there. There I would be in the police station, the apparent bad parent, and there was the child screaming for me. The police must have known something was not right with Brent's portrayal of me. But Brent's bull-like lawyer used every avenue he could to paint me as the villain. By the time Danielle got into Brent's car, I would be completely emotionally drained and devastated. I would drive back to Miami with her cries in my ears, the picture of Brent's cold eyes in my mind, wondering, *why do I let her go to this man?* I didn't think he abused her, but I knew that in her heart she knew he was cruel; much of his fighting for her was to punish me. Children know.

This was why drugs were a very welcome escape for those lonely, haunted weekends. When Danielle was with me, I was mostly sober, going to church and praying rosaries, knowing at least my daughter deserved that. A few months went by, and I found myself needing to find a place to live again. We went to live with a friend named Lupe, a Mexican veterinarian tech. I had met him when I was working as a stripper. He was religious, like me, and this was to be a temporary situation since Lupe's girlfriend, Michelle, was returning to him, and we would need to move out. The fact that this situation was temporary was another gift from God, because Lupe was all about finding ways to escape his pain in ways that I hadn't even known about. His friends had every kind of drug imaginable, and they were always around. One day we were snorting oxycodone while Danielle was with her father. I woke up two days later in a different house, completely naked on the sofa, as people walked in and out. All I remember was being in the bedroom at one point with someone on top of me and inside of me. I didn't think much of it because I had such low self-esteem and took being treated as an object for granted and as a reality. I expected bad things to happen to me. My attitude was that I deserved it for all the things that had gone wrong. I thought I could handle it since bad things seemed to be my middle name.

I never spoke up about these types of travesties; I just accepted that this is what happens with men, and I could not expect anything different. At that time, which was a type of "bottom" for me, there were probably other events that happened that I don't even remember; I just took this kind of behavior in stride. Lupe's girlfriend Michelle was now coming back so Danielle and I had to find another new place to live. I was scared we would have nowhere to go, but Lupe found us housing with one of his good friends, Eddy. He was a sweet, hardworking Spanish guy who extended his apartment to us for several months until I had a boyfriend again. Eddy never expected anything in return or asked me for money. It was refreshing, and I thought maybe it was a sign God was helping me. I met Lupe's girlfriend Michelle, a pretty Spanish girl who had now returned to Lupe with her son. At first, she was suspicious of me, but soon she saw there was nothing between Lupe and me, and we became close friends as two single mothers trying to raise our kids.

I had to work and continue college, which was a slow and frustrating process because of the custody battles. Jay Levy was on top of the legalities, but between the weekend drugs and the continual feeling of being rejected by Mark, I was fighting terrible depression. I just wanted to lie down on a couch with my hair covering my face and never get up. Being alone in the world didn't help. I had friends like Lupe and Michelle and Jennifer, but I did not feel I was part of a base or a family. I would go to mass every morning before I went to college; I placed Danielle in their daycare, where I volunteered so Danielle could go for free while I went to classes. I was still getting A's in almost all my classes, and at least I had that to keep my mind occupied.

My favorite honors class was philosophy. I was beginning to think that I might not want to work as a nurse; they had such long shifts and I remembered my mother never being around when she was working. I liked spending time with Danielle, and I wanted to be able to see her and spend time with her. I was not sure what I would do. I had to extend my studies because of everything I was going through. For example, one time I went to the McDonald's™ across the street from Wolfson campus to eat. I met a nice man who invited me to study with him. It was noisy in the restaurant, and I easily trusted people for some reason, perhaps because I had so much faith that there wasn't anything I couldn't survive. Maybe, like some other victims of PTSD, I unconsciously liked putting myself in dangerous situations; that was when the adrenaline flowed. Also, because I had been through so much, I tended to be compassionate of other people. I knew that each life held much sorrow. Who was I to sit in judgment of anyone? Mostly, since I had never been protected, I did not know how to protect myself. With Jay Levy I was learning a little bit about taking care of myself, but I knew nothing then of putting myself first.

So I walked with this stranger to his house nearby, and he offered me a quiet bedroom where I could study. I thought this was polite and I went in there with my books. Within a minute, he rushed into the bedroom and put his entire weight on top of me, pushing me onto the bed while he spread my legs and pushed my panties and shorts to the side so he could rape me. I was completely shocked; I froze, unfortunately making it easier for him to overpower me. Yet it was also strangely erotic and that shocked me more. It was so quickly, maybe five seconds, before he was done that I came to my senses. I immediately got up, left, and went to a nearby payphone to call the police. I learned that Detective Ellen Christopher never followed up on my call because it was me. Who was going to take me seriously when my file already showed I had been a "liar" with the case with my parents? I never heard anything about it. What was particularly sad about this was that I was sure this man was a serial rapist. There was something too practiced about how he did it.

I had to wonder what this was all about with me. Did I bring this on myself? Was the fact I am very small and feminine looking bring out the brute in men, making them feel as if they are Tarzans physically? Since I had been so sexualized by men, did I give off a come-on vibe? It was confusing to me. Did they sense that I had been sexually abused and think, *what was one more?* I think people do know when someone has been violated or has been weakened, and lesser people are opportunists. I was not overly dramatic when these things happened to me, but they were happening too often. When would it end? I became my own deepest fear. Did I want to be abused? Abusive people can smell this, and I knew enough psychology to know that this can happen. I had been told all my life that I was bad; maybe this was the way I was presenting myself.

I even continued to see Mark on occasion, which only added to my feeling badly about myself. He had broken my heart and he seemed to enjoy the idea of taunting me about it. Did that make him feel bigger? "Maybe you can have me," he seemed to say. And then, he'd follow it up with, "No, you can't." It was like ripping a band-aid off an unhealed wound.

I went back to work at Hooters™ and one of the girls there said, "I have just the thing for your depression." This time she was right, and this is how I started overdoing cocaine. I loved it. It made me feel safe, as though I was hidden in the closet with the presence of God, and nothing mattered. Finally, I had long moments of feeling good. I liked it so much that there was a part of me that wanted to overdose with it and end everything.

Jay Levy was still fighting Brent, but Brent never gave up. Eventually, I began to feel my number would be up and I would lose. Every time I thought about it —losing Danielle after losing everything else I had lost— I wanted to fall asleep and not wake up. I began to have a drive for coke and began taking more, in fact, so much that twice I started having convulsions. This did not frighten me because some part of me thought, *this is what I want: to die.* God does not want me to have a family, He took my other family away, and now He has Brent working tirelessly on taking away Danielle. I might as well let God take me too. The truth was, when I was dying, I saw that I didn't want to die at all. It was Danielle again that kept me alive.

Chapter 16

Dear Lord,
Your love in me is like a flame that burns within my heart,
Giving light to all I do and everything that I am.
Sometimes it dances in my soul as I praise Your name.
At times, it dims or flickers low when hard times come my way.
Even in the darkest hours, I sense your light afresh, reminding me to trust in You.
Be still and wait and rest my soul!
For every flame needs gentle fuel.
Your love is the key,
For keeping this little candle alight in me. It guides my life, my thoughts, my dreams,
And shines for all to see.
Thank You for the happiness and peace you give to me. **Aimee Cabo**

At this time I was in a hotel. Danielle was asleep on the bed. I was with a person who was not a lover or close friend, just a person with whom I was doing cocaine. We had been snorting for three days. It was not the first time that I went into a convulsion, but it could have been the last time. Rather than thrashing and fighting against the convulsion, I felt myself levitating in the air, while I lay flat, feeling complete serenity. Then there was a pitch-black tunnel, and I was in the middle of it; one end of the tunnel was narrow, and one end was wide. It didn't matter which way I was going; I just loved where I was. It didn't matter what I came from; nothing mattered. It was like life was one big fairy tale, a mirage without consequence. The tunnel showed there was a much bigger picture and I had never felt so well or had so much peace in my heart. I felt I was where I belonged. I felt completely changed, not touched by struggle and pain, but free and heavenly. It was just perfect. Everything I had known was erased. This was all a new beginning and there was nothing I wanted or needed. I wanted this moment to continue in this feeling of contentment that I hadn't even believed was possible. I gave myself over and just kept falling more deeply into it. I was sinking away from consciousness and rising higher into something more beautiful. Finally, I was leaving. I kept traveling, lightly and gently, into this new world. Nothing else mattered. I was on my way.

Then I heard as if from a long way away, "Aimee, wake up. Danielle, think of Danielle. Danielle." I could hardly move or raise myself.

"Aimee, Danielle. Come back for Danielle," He began shouting her name, over and over.

I didn't want to leave that tunnel, *but what was going on with Danielle?* I thought. *Is she okay? What has happened?* I struggled to regain consciousness. *Is Danielle alright?* was the only thought in my mind.

"Aimee!" I heard, "Danielle needs you. Wake up!!!"

I forced myself to open my eyes then closed them. Again, I forced myself to open them. I made it. I kept blinking, my mouth was so dry, and I whispered, "What happened to Danielle?"

"Oh fuck," he said, "you were completely blue. Danielle is okay, but I thought we lost you. Jesus."

I couldn't comprehend all that but was still fixated on Danielle. "Where is she?"

"She's asleep," he said. "She's fine, she's been asleep all this time."

I wasn't sure I believed him. Why had he said her name before? I was weak and still half in the other realm. I tried to stand up, but my legs were like spaghetti. I was coming to a little more each moment, and I had to take each step very slowly, then sit down before trying again. Finally, I stood up with a little more equilibrium and saw her sleeping there peacefully. Thankfully, nothing was wrong with Danielle. My friend just knew what to say to get me to come back from the place I had not wanted to return from. He sat on the other bed running his hands through his hair. "Oh my God," he said, completely terrified, "You were blue and had stopped breathing." Slowly I came fully back to myself. I didn't know what universe I was in, but as soon as I got my strength back, I took Danielle, and we went back to Eddy's. As beautiful as that place had been, I knew something had to give. I went back to what had become a normal life, which was anything but normal since I didn't have a place of my own and I kept losing jobs from my depression and pain. As I went through the days, trying to care for Danielle and find us a new place, I deeply regretted leaving that wonderful dark place where everything just seemed to go away, and I got to start all over.

I then knew there was a better place than this earth. I thought, *I must have felt heaven,* when I tried to understand it all, but I believed Danielle needed me and God had given me another chance at life. Eddy said we had to leave the house; he had relatives coming. I completely understood, but this always frightened me. Where would we go? I had no money, and at the time, no boyfriend. Meanwhile, I had put Danielle in the Good Shepherd Catholic pre-school, where I got to know the school social worker, a tall, dark-haired, slender, fairly young man with a soft-spoken voice. There are angels everywhere and he was always kind to me when I dropped her off. Soon, he found out about our desperate situation of having no home and how dangerous that would be with my continual custody battles. He could see how much Danielle and I loved each other.

I came to get her one day and he said, "Aimee! I want you to sign these papers for Section 8 housing, which will be free for you both. You'll have your own place." I had never received government help, but we needed somewhere to go right away. We could not continue moving around. Plus, I was tired of the drugs that seemed to follow us everywhere we moved. I signed the papers.

The Section 8 housing was in a low economic area in Homestead; there were guns and blood in the street, but the apartment building was well kept, and the apartment itself was very clean, which has always been important to me. It was perfect for us. It was a home. We moved there immediately.

I have noticed in my life that people who are struggling are often much more kind to others than those who have everything. Sometimes rich people are isolated in their world, where they can shut their eyes to the tragedies that they only read about in the paper. But those who live with daily life and death struggle have wounded hearts that are open to their families and to others who are struggling. They know what it costs and how an outstretched hand can make all the difference.

To the right of our new home lived two Spanish grandparents who always sat on their porch, looking at everything. They would smile at us and look out for Danielle. My neighbors to the left were a black family with a kind, strong, friendly, giving grandmother named Teresa, who was a nurse. All her grown children and grandchildren lived in the same small apartment with her. One of her sons was a big scary black guy that no one would mess with. In some ways, we all felt protected by him. Teresa's other son had AIDS. He liked to be at my place, and we became friends. I was very poor, and I did not have a job. My neighbors understood this and shared groceries with me when I first moved in. When I did find work, I shared groceries with them. In some way, it felt safe there: there were people to help if needed, people who would look out for us. I continued with my studies, taking care of Danielle, getting jobs off and on, and we felt we had God in our lives again, as well as the blessing of free housing. At night, I would talk with my friends in the building and study. It was then that I would go to bed and pray for a husband, and it was then that Nicole called me out of the blue to go to the Dominican Republic on Michelle's honeymoon package. It was then that I knew forever that God listens to our special prayers

.

Chapter 17

*Keep on asking and you will receive what you ask
for. Keep on seeking, and you will find.
Keep on knocking, and the door will be opened to you.*
Matthew 7:7

Bobby and I, although married, had to live apart for a year and a half before he got papers to come to the US. No matter the circumstances, I was confident that we would survive it.

We talked on the phone daily, but around three months into the marriage, amazed that I was truly loved for the first time, there came a dark moment in my life. I was to go through unusual experiences, tinged with their usual taboos, all thanks to making contact with my family.

My brother Daniel, who was much younger by 6 years and who was Andres' biological son, invited me to go camping with his friend and his friend's doctor-father, who happened to be a friend of my mother. *Why not?* I said to myself. I always wanted to spend time with family and, from since I could remember, I have been restored by nature. I have since come to learn that motherless children often nurture themselves through the purity and embrace of music or the outdoors.

On this camping trip, the doctor-father kept giving me alcoholic drinks. Somehow these drinks made me feel really out of it and sleepy. I ended up falling asleep on my side in his son's tent where I felt his teenage son put something inside of me from behind, but I was too sleepy to wake myself. I don't know if it was his finger or he raped me, but I was aware I just couldn't move. It seemed like his father had drugged my drink.

The next day I felt disgusted because this was a teenager acting out, probably pushing himself inside me and, even worse, with his father's blessing. No matter what happened, I felt violated. I never spoke to them or saw them again. Of course, years later my brother Daniel blamed me, because he had been trained by my mother to see me as the one always in the wrong.

But the whole experience made me ashamed and returned me to all the old negative feelings I had about myself.

I realized, no matter how old you are and how far you have come from your past, seeing family can bring it all back. So once again I was feeling like the sick, worthless, sexualized and available-to-anyone child. It depressed me so much and made me feel so hopeless about myself that I did not contact Bobby for about three or four weeks. I didn't want to talk to anyone and spent time in my darkened room. Bobby must have been confused by my behavior, but I was lost in a mire of my own misery.

He would call and I wouldn't answer. He tried for maybe three weeks while I just lay in the dark thinking that I must be destined to suffer. After Bobby stopped calling me, I felt even more unhappy, even though I was responsible for his own feelings of rejection.

I was so lost I started to convince myself I must have liked the doctor who drugged me, but I immediately felt it was wrong and acknowledged to myself I was married.

Then, in my depression, my twisted logic began telling me, if you are thinking about this doctor, then Bobby must be thinking about another woman. After all, he had stopped calling me and all I had known all my life was unfaithful men. This thinking was a bit crazy on my part, since I was the one who did not answer the phone, but I just wanted to stay in the dark and believe he must be in the dark, too. Aside from school and custody battles, I kept to myself and in my own very mixed-up mind.

Somehow, after two months, I suddenly woke up healthy. Maybe God had spoken to me. *What am I doing?* I asked myself. *I am ignoring my handsome, wonderful, kind husband.*

I immediately called him. "Bobby, I love you. I just got a break from school. I have been working so hard. I am so sorry I have been out of touch. Can I come down now and visit?"

"Aimee," he said, "this is not such a good time to come."

Immediately, I got suspicious. "Why not?"

"I too am finishing up some stuff. Come in a month or so."

"No, Bobby, I can't come then because of school. I need to come now."

He hesitated a bit, and then said, "Okay, I will send you a ticket."

Thank God, life is back to normal, I thought. *Thank you, God. I would see Bobby, my love.* I found someone to watch Danielle and planned to apologize to Bobby about my silence when we met. I was sure we would talk about it and work it out. He was good that way. He had always listened and tried to understand.

I arrived, we hugged, he seemed better-looking than ever, and I felt so happy to be with someone I could trust. We went out to lunch by the water and we began talking about our future. I wanted to make some notes for what to get for him at my place. I reached inside his briefcase for a pen and touched a photograph. I had given him one of Danielle and me.

I pulled it out with the pen but to my surprise it was a picture of a Dominican woman with her child. It had writing on the back which read, "Love like this only happens once in a lifetime."

"What is this?" I asked, my stomach turning.

"What?" he asked.

I put my hand in his briefcase looking for Dani's and my picture. Nothing.

"Where's our picture?"

"Must be at home."

"What is this picture?" I asked again, holding the one of the Dominican woman.

"Oh, I don't know how that picture ended up in my briefcase."

"What do you mean?" I asked, trying to keep my voice neutral.

Then I tried a new tack. "I understand," I said. "After all, we both live alone at this point and people think we're free because we're not together. I guess these things are normal in long distance situations."

Bobby immediately relaxed when he saw I wasn't going crazy.

"Yes," he said, "I have been seeing this woman. It's been strange. I love you but I also love her." He put his hands through his hair. "In fact, I got totally confused. I don't know who I love."

I thought about how he hadn't wanted me to come now. *He must love her.* I looked at him, tears coming to my eyes, but I was trying to hide them. I knew I still loved him, *but maybe he doesn't love me.*

Now, I couldn't contain myself and burst out angrily, "If you don't know who you love, you can't possibly love either of us. Doesn't a person only love one person at a time?"

"Aimee, I never had sex with her."

"Bobby, who cares? If you felt you might be in love with her, it IS an affair. A full-fledged affair."

Now I was really crying. He doesn't love me. He is the only man I ever wholeheartedly wanted. God had ordained this marriage. What is going on here?

Bobby reached over, "But Aimee, it is nothing with her. We just got close because I didn't know what to think of us, since I haven't been able to get in touch with you. Didn't you like a doctor in Miami?"

"But I didn't get close with him. I stayed away. If you really do care at all about me and this marriage, you have to call her and end this affair or whatever it is immediately."

I needed to know he loved me more than her, or I felt I would die.

He didn't pull out his phone. Nothing.

Bobby looked completely confused. He didn't want to call her, especially at this moment, but there I was, sobbing uncontrollably because he was hesitating. Again, I thought, *Bobby loves her. I can't go through this.*

"If you love me," I sobbed and said again, "you must call her. Why aren't you calling her?"

"I don't want to break her heart."

I cried even more. *What about hurting me,* I thought. *Why does everyone hurt me?*

What should I do? I thought, as I saw him struggling with himself. Should I walk away from my marriage…my dreams shattered. My life in Miami is only difficulty, and now this. I believed I was his everything, as he was to me, that our love was anointed by God and our relationship blessed and unique, but here was another woman claiming that their love was special.

Bobby finally pulled out his phone in front of me, called the woman, and told her he was married and could not continue the relationship. She hung up on him. I sat there devastated. I tried to think. Bobby had been chosen by God for me. He had given me the sign. The devil must have got to him, taken advantage of him because he was lonely, and allowed his soul to be seduced by someone.

Bobby just sat there with a sad look on his face. I ran outside, unable to contain my emotions, crying. *God wouldn't break my heart,* I told myself. *This is my soul mate. I must stick to it, continue to trust God. I must love him unconditionally.* Bobby had run after me. *Bobby did the right thing by calling her. Focus on the good, I told myself,* as he caught up to me and I saw that he now looked stronger. He had fought the devil.

He hugged me, wiping the tears from my face, and assured me that we would be okay.

"Ok," I replied and looked at him, still with tears in my eyes.

We had a few more days together before I was to go back.

"Aimee, you are the one, and we should put this behind us," he said later at dinner.

I thought, *Okay, I want this to work. I'll trust God and make the best out of our time since it is so limited and pretend it never happened.*

It did go through my mind that his decision between that woman and me might have been easy: a new life in Miami or stay stuck in the Dominican Republic making no money? I would have chosen me too.

Then I would run to his defense in my mind. Nobody is a saint, I told myself, even though as a child I had wanted to be one myself.

No, have faith, I told myself. *Trust God on this one. God doesn't make mistakes.* It wasn't easy for me to forgive, since he admitted he'd almost left me. He hadn't wanted me to come, meaning he preferred to stay with her. Somehow, I knew it had been a real affair, even though he wouldn't give me any details. I made the choice to focus on his good parts, the beauty in him. I told myself God really is the cure for everything. I stayed with him.

We still had another year to be apart, and this woman would be there in DR, but I kept reminding myself it was me whom he married legally.

I decided we would enjoy our next two days and I would let it go. And I did.

I returned to Miami and never said a thing to him or anyone else about what happened; I decided to do whatever it would take to help our long distance relationship survive. I regained control of my feelings and continued with the life of school, Danielle, and moving forward.

Deep down I knew in my heart that if love is meant to be, and the person you love is right for you, nothing can stop that love.

We never had an incident like that again over the next year-and-a-half that Bobby and I had to wait to be together. Finally, he was able to come to the US legally.

A few days before he was to arrive, I decorated the apartment with welcome signs and love paraphernalia and my husband whom, in truth, I hardly knew, moved in to our one-bedroom Section 8 apartment in Homestead, FL. That is when we really got to know one other. He met the neighbors and we were so excited to be together that we didn't mind that we were living in a tiny place. I took him all over Miami and we just took joy in being together.

During one dinner I said, "Can you believe we are this happy and we got married and didn't even know each other?"

He laughed and said, "I know. Not to mention, that moving fast is not like me at all."

"What do you mean?"

"I was engaged before, you know."

My heart sank. Not again. He loved someone else. Well, of course he did. I had thought I loved Mark.

"What happened?" I asked.

"I was engaged for four years when I lived in Bulgaria."

"Why didn't you marry her?" I asked, grabbing my drink a little tighter.

He looked at me and said, "She died from a mysterious stomach problem."

How horrible, I thought, *to have someone you love die*. I didn't think I could survive his or Danielle's death. I knew I could survive much suffering, but not that. I said a prayer sitting there: Dear God, I will endure any suffering that comes my way, but please don't ever let me suffer the death of a loved one.

"It was terrible, Aimee," he said, "but I am happy with my life now. I am thrilled to be with you. It was what was meant to happen, so all things work out the way they are supposed to." Then he flashed me one of those big laughing smiles.

And this is why I love this man, I thought. *He too looks at things with a long vision and he, too, believes in the goodness of life.*

Bobby and I did not seem to have a difficult time adjusting to the newness of each other or marriage, but Danielle was different. She didn't like this interloper.

To make matters worse, she had always slept in my bed. I explained to her that this had to change.

"I don't see why," she said, in her own bed, as I tucked her in. "You belong to me. We've always been together."

"We are still together, but you're almost eight; you should sleep in your own bed. You're growing up. You're a big girl. And…I am still yours," I said, "but now we are with him, too. He is a good father, you will see."

"I was happy just the two of us," she said. "I don't want him telling me what to do."

"Me neither," I laughed. "I don't want him telling me what to do either, but he is not that type, you'll see."

I kissed her good night, confident that they would grow easy with each other.

And just like I was, Danielle soon found herself enchanted with this man who made her laugh with his jokes, who listened to her seriously when she talked about the dramas with school friends or what was going on with her, and she grew more and more comfortable with him when she saw how he never yelled or was unkind to her.

I knew we were all in good stead when she came to me in the kitchen one day and said, "My new dad is pretty cool; you're right."

I practically started dancing.

Bobby is a natural parent, with a great sense of humor. Bobby likes kids because he had previously worked as a pediatrician in Bulgaria and once had his own upscale private elementary 1-8th grade middle school. Danielle now had the father I always hoped she'd have.

One of our first adventures was taking her horseback riding and I had never seen her so happy. I could see the sun and trust begin to infuse her face.

One night when she was asleep, I told Bobby, "I am so grateful you are good with her. She has been through a lot. Her father is not a nice person and she knows it. She is blossoming, I can see that, with your love."

"Of course, I love her, she is part of you."

The three of us now were always doing something together. We went to amusement parks and he seemed to enjoy the rides as much as she did. They both saw eating junk food as fun. He made up games in the car, and he communicated in a warm, teasing, holding way.

He even brought out the kid in me, the kid who had never been allowed to be a kid. I found myself laughing and teasing and just being goofy. I felt safe. I felt he would never hurt me, ever, and there are no words to express what that meant for me.

It would do nothing less than change my DNA. To be with someone I could share everything with was giving me a stability and home I had never had.

Bobby proved to be someone I could lean on and count on; he was extremely reliable, responsible and always available. Most important, he was understanding, and for the first time in my life, I felt truly loved.

This changed everything for me.

Add to that, I now had my sisters Michelle and Nicole in my life again after so many years. I especially grew close to Michelle, for she understood in a deep way what I had gone through, the abuse and being ridiculed for it. She too had been sacrificed to my mother's insistence to the world that Andres was innocent and Michelle and I were the ones who were crazy. What we had experienced with that man was of no interest to my mother. It was a vicious abandonment that both Michelle and I did not have to discuss but were able to see in the dark recesses of each other's eyes.

Michelle turned out to be amazingly kind and we made up for the lost time when we hadn't seen each other because we'd both been too lost to our private hells. But now we would take trips to Miramar to visit with each other and Danielle got to know her cousins, Kaitlin, Steven, Matthew, and especially Ricky, who was only three months apart from Danielle and was a natural born comedian. Matthew was the tough guy who was really a sweetheart and Steven was the highly intelligent patriotic one. The baby of the family was Kaitlin, Michelle's only daughter, and she turned out to be extremely cool, individualistic and clever, besides being blonde and beautiful like her mother. I was happy for Michelle that she finally got a girl, just before tying her tubes.

At the time I had an old Honda that Bobby used to get to his first job as a medical assistant for an insurance company and advising on settlements. This car also took us to church, or therapy and school for Danielle and me. The three of us operated as the ideal, hardworking family, and now I found myself completely sober. No drugs, no drink. I didn't need it. My heart was full and my loneliness and anxiety relieved. There was no inner void that was hurting me.

Bobby was working many hours and I was going to school while Danielle attended elementary school. Now that I was mentally balanced, I was in the last part of my education at Miami Dade Community College, and I had saved all the hard classes, like statistics, for the end. I had the stamina, support, and mental health to do so.

Brent and his terrible lawyer kept coming after me, but Jay Levy had them under control and the story to tell the judges about me was getting more and more benign. They were running out of horror stories.

There wasn't a day that I did not sit down in our Section 8 housing apartment in a rough part of town and tell God how grateful I was and how blessed I felt to have such an amazing, supportive, loving family, one I had always dreamed of having.

Danielle now had two parents on her mother's side, two aunts and four cousins. God had answered my prayers. I had always wanted better for her.

Little does my precious Saint Bobby know the life he has got himself into, I'd sometimes think. I had nothing to offer him but my love and the baggage that came with us, but he never seemed to mind. It turned out he was the kind of person who trusted his soul and was an extremely hard worker and always willing to give of himself. He never withheld. He became my best friend and helped me with the custody case, with my schooling when I needed it, with childcare, you name it. It was no longer Danielle and me alone against the world, fighting to stay together. Three of us was a better number and, as Danielle and I saw it, God sent a new sheriff to town.

Chapter 18

Every word you give me is a miracle word— How could I help but obey?
Break open your words, let the light shine out, Let ordinary people see the meaning.
Psalm 119:130

Bobby was all about progress. As quickly as he united our lives, he upgraded our lives. Not even a year went by before Bobby moved us out of Homestead to a three-bedroom duplex he had purchased in Cutler Ridge. This home had a small wood-fenced backyard, a large living room, and came complete with a washer and dryer. I had never had a home of my own, let alone a home where I was safe. On the day, as we were leaving the Homestead apartment, I saw a large pool of fresh human blood on the wall across from my door. *We're moving out in the nick of time,* I thought, as I realized what a dangerous place Danielle and I had been living in. For all the time we were there, it was as if I had been walking around with blinders; I was oblivious to the dangers of our surroundings because I believed everything was in God's hands. We had to love our Section 8 home, and we did. I had shut my eyes to the reality of it because I always tried to look at the positive and this free housing had been a lifesaver for us. Of course, I was no stranger to danger. I knew how to shut down so as not to feel fear. Those days were coming to an end.

We were excited to move to Cutler Ridge, and once we moved, there now began a series of amazing gifts. First, Danielle and Bobby got to watch me graduate from Miami Dade with honors and distinction, all accomplished while I had battled homelessness, drugs, poverty, humiliating and unending custody battles, heartbreak, and severe depression. Like Churchill, thought, I never, never, never gave up. So, as I wore my cap and gown in the Miami sun, I had to give myself credit for making it. For believing in the good, just as I had when I met Bobby. For not letting the dark side, that bull, win. For knowing what was right and wrong. For being a model to my daughter. For seeing that faith works. My next stop would be the University of Miami where I would begin nursing studies.

The fact I was married now didn't deter Brent and Candy from continually filing motions against us for a change of custody. Now we could pay Jay Levy at a discounted rate, but it seemed like bringing me to court and slandering me was a way of life for Brent and Candy. Jay kept suppressing their motions, but it was still exhausting, expensive, humiliating in ways, and absolutely a waste of everyone's time and money. At this point, it was about pride for Brent and Candy and pride eventually comes to a fall. Unfortunately, it would take time before they and their pride fell down entirely.

Bobby and I continued experiencing our life together as a fairy tale. All we saw was each other. We loved each other so much that three years later, I made a suggestion: "Why don't we get married again in a Catholic Church? A proper marriage." Bobby was Eastern Orthodox, and we were both realizing that our respective religions had similarities. There are seven sacraments in the Eastern Orthodox and Roman Catholic Churches. These include baptism, reconciliation/penance, confirmation, communion, marriage, holy orders and the anointing of the sick. However, the Eastern Orthodox use unleavened bread, while the Catholics use leavened bread. Priests may marry (although not Bishops) in Eastern Orthodoxy, which is, of course, different from Roman Catholicism but, otherwise, the actual services are very similar. For Bobby, none of this mattered. He wasn't the religious type anyway, but like me, he was a romantic.

"Where?" he asked.

I said, "The Gesu Catholic Church." "Why?" he asked.

"It is a beautiful large antique church in downtown Miami," I said. "Both my sisters and all my friends from college can come. It can be a real wedding. The real thing," I said, excitedly. Many women have somewhere in their mind that "white wedding fantasy" when they are queen for a day. He saw how much it meant to me.

"Let's do it," he said.

On December 13, 2003, I was ready in my floor-length, sophisticated, sequined wedding dress with a long train. The church was full of our friends, my fellow students, and Jennifer and Danielle standing by to walk me down the aisle. Bobby stood waiting at the front of the church. After two hours of standing there, the priest, Father Leo Leise, said to Bobby, "I'm not waiting much longer." I hadn't shown up.

"She'll be here," Bobby said. He was sure I wanted to remarry him, but he had no idea what happened.

What happened was that my sisters forgot we had to go to a wedding and the limo got lost and never came. I finally arrived at the church door in Michelle's pickup truck with all of us in it and my long white train hanging out of the window. The singer, who was ill, had also waited patiently. When I arrived, she began singing *Ave Maria* just as I was making my way down the aisle to my wonderful husband, who was annoyed and exhausted from worrying and having to stand there so long. We said our vows, and mishaps and all, it was another one of the happiest days of my life. I now felt this marriage was sealed with God's kiss.

Meanwhile, Bobby had begun working for himself, setting up a business where the insurance companies came to him, rather than being on their salary; of course, he did it better. This was classic Bobby, seeing an opportunity and building upon it. He was proactive. Soon after this, like the new wife I was, I became pregnant. We were so happy. There was no one I wanted to have a baby with more. Bobby has excellent genetics and so many outstanding qualities. He is such a kind and sensitive man. It made sense when I discovered one of his great-grandfather's distant relatives had been a saint in Bulgaria. Saint Neophit Rilski, from the Rila monastery, was a 19th-century monk, teacher, and artist. In fact, Saint Rilski created the first grammar book of the modern Bulgarian language, and he made the first popular translation of the entire Bible in the modern Bulgarian language. So, we know where Bobby's intelligence and flair with languages comes from!

We both were elated with this pregnancy (another saint, I prayed!), but soon after, I miscarried. I cried and cried. I wanted so much for us to be a family. During this period of our second wedding, moving to a new house, and the new pregnancy, I kept attending the University of Miami, working toward a Bachelor of Science in nursing and a minor in psychology. Naturally, we were still going through custody battles with Brent and Candy, but since my life was stable now, these were more of an annoyance and expense than a fear. God has always been good to me, and before Bobby and I knew it, we were greatly blessed again.

Two years later, in 2005, our first child, Sean, was born. I hadn't had any labor pains with Danielle, so I decided to give birth naturally without any type of anaesthesia. Nicole and Michelle were present. I had chosen to deliver Sean at Baptist Hospital because my estranged sister Jeanette was a labor and delivery nurse there and I hoped to have the opportunity to see her and rekindle our relationship. I hadn't seen her since we were kids. I had gambled right; Jeanette must have seen my name on the delivery roster and decided to show up on her day off to help deliver Sean. With him, I was all belly and he weighed in at eight pounds, four ounces.

I had asked to have the television on in my room to distract me from the intense labor pains and the burial of Pope John Paul II was airing; he was canonized a saint by Pope Francis. Since Pope John Paul was doing me the kindness of helping me with my delivery, at the last minute, I decided I would add "Paul" to Sean's name in his memory, since the name Sean also means John. Once I had reached eight centimeters of dilation, I changed my decision about natural childbirth. Having violently projectile vomited three times from the searing pain immediately following an intense, prolonged contraction, I begged for an epidural. The epidural was such a relief, but I could still feel the pressure. I went into a hypotension crisis due to the anaesthesia being administered late.

The nurses began telling me, "Get on your knees." There must have been ten people in the room, and they were trying to kick Bobby out, maybe in preparation in case they had to do surgery. I felt exhausted and I just wanted to go to sleep, but Bobby stayed there and begged me not to close my eyes. They stabilized me and Sean Paul was born within five minutes, given the very strong contractions as I pushed and with the doctor's brilliant maneuver in getting Sean's shoulder unstuck.

While nursing my baby as I insisted I would, I graduated from the University of Miami with a B average. This freed up my time to take care of my infant son, which was something new for me. I felt like a first-time mother after twelve years of not having a baby. I loved spending time with Sean so much that I didn't even pursue working as a nurse. I didn't want to be an absentee mom like my mother had been for me. I couldn't even stand to hear him cry. Anytime I felt his feelings were hurt, I would pick him up and comfort him. It seemed he was always in my arms. I even showered while carrying him.

Bobby was very helpful and supportive in every way, and there was not a thing in the outside world I had to worry about. Yet I would be riddled with overwhelming sadness at times, which I tried my best to ignore. I wasn't self-medicating, and I was still going to therapy with Dr. Lopez-Brignoni. My best friend Jennifer had found her soulmate at the same time I did and we'd both slowed down our previously fast-paced lives. Now, we spent time together as couples.

On one hand, I was happier than I had ever been. There was my precious Danielle and there were two males I deeply loved Sean and Bobby. I had a home, accomplishments, and stability, all assets I had never had before. But I found that I woke up with constant stomach pain from an inner stress I couldn't quite figure out and I often felt deeply bereft and saw no reason to live. That childhood wound felt so deep that it simply left a knife in my body. I could ignore it, but there were times I just had to lay down; I would feel like I never wanted to get up. In 2007, we visited Bobby's family in Bulgaria. Sofia, the capital, is at the foot of the Vitosha Mountain and surrounded by high Balkan Mountains on every side. The city is fairly close to the Aegean Sea. I was struck by the city's blend of mixed heritage antiquity of Hungarian, Ottoman, and Bulgarian origins, due to different occupations—coupled with its modernity. Sofia is considered one of the top ten places in the world for start-up businesses; it also is considered one of the most affordable capitals to live in.

Bobby and I had already decided to get married again while we were there, while pregnant with my third child, this time for his family in an Eastern Orthodox Church by a priest who was a friend of Bobby's father. The church we chose for the ceremony was the ancient Saint George Church. Bobby's father, an unusually tall, kind, loving, gentle giant, and his mom, a high-spirited, pretty, short-haired brunette with a wit like Bobby's, were proud and loving to us both, and they officiated as hosts at this wedding. Bobby even had his high school and medical school friends there, and it was very festive. His Aunt Ivona was my maid of honor. The wedding was performed by three priests in a traditional and formal manner with incense, as we stood there in the huge cathedral.

The party and celebration were welcoming and joyous, but of course, I couldn't understand any of the language with its totally different alphabet. I have since learned to read it, but I find it very hard to speak. A year later, Sean was a toddler and began attending Montessori school down the street from us. It was there that we discovered that Sean was highly intelligent. I felt he had got that from his father's side and my mother's family.

In 2007, I became pregnant with a little girl. I was so happy. It was a full-term pregnancy; I was overweight and had pre-eclampsia. The doctor gave me a medication that made me feel sleepy or like I had the flu. I was also on an oxytocin drip to induce labor. A doctor rushed in just in time; as soon as I opened my legs, the tiniest baby slid out asleep, without my even pushing. She was born in January, and we named her after my closest sister Michelle. She needed to be revived, and once she came to, the little girl was precious, and I was immediately in love. Once she came home, Sean and Danielle adored her too. Michelle, like Sean, was always in my arms. I had to wean Michelle from breastfeeding at two years old, unlike Sean who lost interest when he turned one.

Michelle was a beautiful, small child with a unique personality. She had a sweet and lively way about her, but sometimes she would say things that were off the wall and her learning milestones were slower than her brother's. Eventually, once she completed pre-school, we decided to test her genetically and discovered she had 3q29 microdeletion syndrome. This means that when all the chromosomes were fused together, there was one micro piece deleted at the third chromosome. She could have been born with a cleft lip and clubfoot, as well as having all her organs affected with this syndrome. We checked all her organs for abnormalities, just to be sure, and none were noted.

Even though Michelle has a pixie-like appearance and some strange ways of looking at things (who doesn't?), she is completely normal. The only thing I noticed was that she needed more practice with her studies and trial and error reinforcement from us at home. Bobby and I, as always, worked together on this.

I got pregnant three more times after Michelle was born, between the time that I was thirty-six and thirty-seven years old. All three pregnancies occurred during this two-year period. The first two miscarriages were early miscarriages, and we knew the third child had died when we saw no heartbeat at two months. I refused a DNC and carried the fetus for four months before I naturally released it. I was able to bury it, but I became seriously septic and almost died.

This was all very sad, but it also tells me that the children I do have are miracles. We love them all the more because of it. Then Bobby gave me the sweetest gift. Years ago, Bobby had helped me replace my missing tooth, but now, because my breasts had lost shape because of all the breastfeeding, he got me beautiful youthful breasts with a well-known plastic surgeon, a luxurious gift I had never expected. We were happy and our family was fulfilled. We also knew we could get through sadness together, but that bull from my childhood dream doesn't like happiness. He is not used to it and he does not admire it. He likes trouble and destruction. He wanted to make a reappearance. I had to remind myself that, in my childhood dream, that bull finally settles down.

Chapter 19

Danielle was now fourteen years old and asserted with the energy of her teenage defiance that she didn't want to see her father on weekends. I was not going to force her. She was no longer a young child that needed adults to speak on her behalf. In the old days, I would make her go to her father's house so that Brent and Candy could not use that against me. I never liked her going there because I could see she was not happy, but it was what I had to do legally. But now Danielle had grown strong, and she had learned to protect herself. She had also blossomed with the stability of Bobby's and my love, as well as Bobby's kindness to her. She had a solid, reliable, healthy base; all Brent's insults of me didn't ring true to her. It was now our home that emanated a healthy and joyous lifestyle.

We saw a large house in Palmetto Bay with a pool, jacuzzi, and three bedrooms. I asked God: *If I can only know what it's like to live in a house like this, even if only for a short time, it would be so wonderful.* What I thought was impossible became possible. Bobby bought us this house, and, for the first time, we had a dream home and everything we needed. The house had been built in the 1970s; it was full of mirrors, lots of windows, and there were graceful glass

French doors. Yet the best part for me was the backyard. It was an oasis of nature with tropical landscaping of palm trees, lilies, irises, begonias, and the most beautiful huge old tree I'd ever seen. Old trees are spiritual to me, as if they have ultimate wisdom and can cast spells upon people.

We wanted for nothing. The five of us were one great, happy family and everyone had their own room. Then 2008 hit and the economy went into a kind of shock, with huge banks failing and everyone worrying about their income. President Obama came to office, and in my opinion, he had no idea how to pull the economy out of its seismic shock. The business my husband was struggling to build, as with so many businesses, came to a standstill. Nobody wanted to spend any money or fund any industry.

Then I began to do something that people who are facing financial challenges often do; we become defiant. We were suffering financially, and I wanted to refuse limits. I began to spend a lot of money. I'd buy expensive clothes for the children and buy things for myself. I would just spend. Shopping gave me something to look forward to. The glitter of the expensive shops, the way they treat you as if you are royalty, all made me forget that we didn't have enough money. I went for it.

Bobby said, "You have to stop this, Aimee. We can't do it." "But I feel so hemmed in."

"Do something else," he said.

When I stopped shopping, I started to feel my depression intensify and begin to creep its way back into my head and body. I could almost not handle the feelings of emptiness and grief. I was edgy and unhappy, and I felt the house would come crumbling down, with our pressures and the pressures inside me. The house wasn't going to come crumbling down; it was me who was about to come crumbling down. All the pain of my youth came flying back in. In truth, it m probably, had never left, but I had been able to distract myself.

Children, building a business, moving into a new home —all of that can keep you so busy you can forget your own demons and not deal with the parts of yourself that you need to pay attention to. That bull of my dream now did a clever thing to get his way. He sent Lupe and his drug friends back into my life. "Hi Aimee, how is it going?" Lupe said on the phone.

And in my feelings of loneliness and desperation, I went for the call.

Now Bobby was not only frightened of his business going down the drain, but also that his wife, with these kinds of friends, might go down the drain, too. I started leaving the house for hours and visiting with Lupe, who lived in a world of druggie friends. I met "B," who took me to his apartment where he cooked large amounts of pure cocaine that he turned into crack in the microwave. "Try it," he said. "You won't believe what it's like."

I was in so much pain —my body was physically wracked by it, even though it was an emotional pain— that I tried his crack. The euphoria is ten times more intense than what you feel with cocaine, but the euphoria is also very short, which creates a terrible craving to do more of it. I would come home, a little craven, a little high.

Bobby would anxiously say, "What's up with you Aimee? You okay?"

"Yes, yes," I'd say. "I just smoked a little weed with Lupe. I'll be fine in a little bit."

He'd look at me a little quizzically, but when you want to believe something, you believe it. Bobby was no different. And he was fighting his own problems. I knew he was busy dealing with economic challenges, and I did not want to ask him for money for more crack, but without it, my old misery and feeling of not wanting to live were in full swing again. Even with the children, I could not prevent these feelings from returning. I started to go off to see B every day. Sometimes he would give me a hit out of kindness, and I would, for a moment, feel pure and up; this became the only state

I wanted to be in. Still, I felt responsible enough to return home daily. Bobby would watch me. He sensed something was different, but drug addicts always think we can fool everyone. We can't. I needed that drug now and B knew it. The more I needed it, the more worthless I felt; the more worthless I felt, the more I needed the high. I'd show up, my eyes and body hungry for it. B would say, "You need a hit, don't you?"

"Yes," I'd answer him.

"Any money?" I'd shake my head.

"Aimee, I am not Santa Claus. But there is a way to get those hits without money," B would say, his eyes taking me in. He didn't even have to say what that way was. I, who love Bobby more than anything, agreed to sex because I had to get out of that excruciating pain, that excruciating deprivation of needing to be somewhere else. I knew this was horrible, a breaking of my vows, but I had no control of myself. The crack had me. By this time, Bobby had figured out what was going on.

"Lupe is giving you drugs, right?" he said when I came home

one evening.

I nodded with tears in my eyes. "Not Lupe, but a friend of his." "What kind of drugs?"

"Crack."

He stood up, began walking quickly back and forth in the living room and said, "Oh, Aimee…" I began to cry.

"What can I do Aimee?" he said, looking as devastated as I had ever seen him.

"If you give me money, I can at least do it at home," I said, still crying, shaking my head. He listened quietly and then looked at me. He must have seen a sorry sight, drugged, hurting, and out of control. He probably thought, *better she is safe here doing this than out on the streets.*

He nodded his head to me and agreed, "Okay, Aimee, do it here." While Bobby might have felt more in control with this situation, we had opened something that would not be good for either of us. Doing crack in the open, so to speak, took limits off me, so my craving for the drug became stronger. I did not have to moderate and hide it. My plan was that I would wait until the kids were asleep and, hating myself, do crack in the closet. I had to do it every night so another bad side effect was that we were becoming more broke. Now I had Bobby traveling my downward spiral with me and he was not happy. Once I came down from the drug, I'd turn to Bobby in the living room and say, "I am such a terrible person."

Bobby would say, "Not true. You're a good person." "You just say that because you love me."

"Yes, I love you," he would answer, "but that's not why I am saying it. You are a good person. I see how you have struggled through everything and tried to do the right thing. I see you love the kids. I see you love me. I see the good in you, Aimee." But I did not believe him or anyone who seemed to like me. I thought if people were kind to me or warm or generous, they were just being polite. I didn't believe their compliments; I thought everyone could see how needy and hurt and weak I felt inside. I thought that was the only thing anyone could see of me. I totally ignored that there were other parts of me, the loving and constant mother and wife, the creative person, the loving person. I thought I was the drug.

While high, I would often pray: *God, release me from this torture.* And that's when I got a very strange answer. We were sitting down at night after feeding the kids and I said to Bobby, "Don't you miss working as a doctor?"

"I do," he said.

"Why don't we go to Bulgaria? You can work at what you love and be with your family and I… I can get away from this." After all, I thought, this is what Miles Davis did to get over heroin. He just left New York and the scene and went cold turkey in some small town in the south where no one knew him, and he didn't know any dealers. It was hard, but it worked.

Bobby looked at me and smiled. "Bingo. Great idea, Aimee. I told you that you would come through." He must have been longing for home during all this and he must have wanted to get me away from everyone and everything.

I smiled, saying, "I've been praying for a release from here."

"Me too," he said. "I've been praying for a solution and I'm not even religious," he laughed. Then Bobby, who never procrastinates, got one-way tickets to Bulgaria for all of us except Danielle who was now sixteen years old. He got her a roundtrip ticket as she was old enough to return to Miami and live with either of my two sisters if she wanted to. We moved so fast it was like we were in the witness protection program. We each took one suitcase, leaving whatever we owned to be sold in a garage sale by Nicole, who was now a realtor. We told her, "Take anything," so she could rent the house for us. All we took with us were a few clothes and some photographs. I did not quite know what I was doing, but I knew I was leaving the drug and getting away from what the Anonymous programs call "people, places, and things." I knew that we would start over. Bobby would be a doctor, and I would be with him and the children. That was all I wanted anyway.

I should be able to manage, I told myself. The morning we were going to leave for Bulgaria, Danielle was not around. "Where is she?" I asked Bobby. I kept calling her cell phone until, finally she answered.

"We're leaving," I said. "Where are you?" She hesitated. "What happened?" I asked.

"My dad came to pick me up last night to say goodbye," she said, and he won't let me go to Bulgaria. He took my passport." She was crying.

"Why did he do that?"

"He says I don't speak the language. There is nothing for me there."

"What do you want to do?" We didn't have time for court injunctions.

"I guess I should stay. What else can I do?"

I have never been a believer in forcing anyone to do anything they don't want to do, so I told her I loved her, and said that when we got there, I would deal with him about the passport and try and get her to come. I also knew she had a boyfriend she didn't want to leave, so maybe part of that was playing into this, but I definitely would have to fight with Brent once again to let her come if she wanted to.

"I love you too, Mom," she said.

"Of course," I said, "and if you change your mind and I get the passport, we have a ticket for you. We are always here."

"I know, Mom."

I said, "And we'll be back before you know it." That afternoon we were on a plane to Bulgaria.

Chapter 20

O Lord,

You are my navigation, A
voice to guide my way.
Such help on every journey,
Within my heart, you reign.
You are my compass, You
lead me to where to go. Even
when the path is dim, Your
truths light all I know.
You are my lighthouse.
In the high seas and storms,
I do not fear the rocks of life,
Your love keeps me warm.
Amen. **Unknown**

Michelle was almost two years old, and Sean was four years old when we landed in Sofia, each of us with our single suitcase. I simply followed Bobby everywhere since, for one thing, I found the language difficult to understand. It felt like I'd landed in an alien land, not to mention the weather was completely different than sunny Miami. The weather can be grey and cold; immediately my body felt like there wasn't enough of me to keep me warm.

Bobby found a job in the countryside of Sevlievo, where we were placed in a rent-free, two-bedroom apartment that the hospital provided; they paid very little money, and we didn't come with much anyway. I was to find myself a long way from my beautiful home in Latino, music-filled Miami. Instead of restaurants and shopping centers, I was now surrounded by cows and goats and shop owners I couldn't understand, who mostly had goods that I was not used to eating or using to cook. Wherever I looked, I saw lots of empty land everywhere. Our two-bedroom apartment had a small hallway for a living room and a tiny kitchen so, in addition, we went from spaciousness to being cramped. That didn't particularly bother me because I can never be close enough to my family.

Since we were in the countryside and almost no one there spoke English, I couldn't make friends. I didn't have my sister and I didn't have Danielle. There was no one for me to talk to; even my children were speaking Bulgarian to each other. Bobby was the only person I could speak English with unless we travelled to the city where Bobby's parents lived. Bobby had found a job at Akta Medika Hospital in Sevlievo, so he was away from home a lot. I was isolated without enough money to go into the city since the salary of a doctor in Bulgaria is minimal.

It took me forever to adjust to the different weather and the lack of central heating, so I took to drinking a lot of beer. For one thing, it warmed me up; second, it took the edge off my loneliness. This was a strange thing for me to do since I have always been petite and conscientious about keeping my shape. Beer is the absolute worst alcohol for that and each month I put on three pounds or more; that added up quickly on my five-foot, one-inch frame. *Since no one saw or talked to me, what difference did it make?* And I must state that I instantly had broken the craving for crack. It seems as soon as I went onto a new plan that occupied my mind, I did not need or want it. So that part of our plan had worked wonderfully.

I tried making sense of the passport business with Brent so Danielle could come to visit, but we all knew this was a lost cause. I heard from her frequently and I learned she was making friends with my brother Daniel, Andres' son, and Daniel's wife, Beatriz. Daniel had been my favorite among my youngest siblings, and he was close in age to Danielle. I could understand her wanting some family connection, even though I was pretty sure they didn't have a kind word for me; none of the family ever did. I played the role of the scapegoat, but I was glad that at least someone was watching out for her.

Meanwhile, Bobby, as noted, was not one to stand still when there are no opportunities for growth. He did not like having his income capped so low. He decided to become an entrepreneur at the hospital. Bulgaria was a good place for start-ups: people were educated, worked hard, could speak multiple languages (in the city), and did not expect large sums of money at the beginning. Bobby opened a medical research facility for pharmaceutical trials for a variety of drugs being tested for many different illnesses. Drug trials are long and complicated and need to be assiduously monitored and coordinated throughout different countries and medical facilities. It was a true career, a huge step for us, and a lucrative one we continued being involved in when we returned to the US.

Since he was building a business, I started a part-time job as a coordinator there so I could be productive too, and we enjoyed working together. During one of her calls, Danielle told us, as I had expected, that she'd run away from her father's house. In typical Brent fashion, he took me to court again claiming that I had abandoned her. Somehow, he was able to get sole custody legally in an *ex parte* motion and hearing. Maybe it was because I was not there to fight, but it was too late now for Brent's antics anyway. Danielle was of an age where what Brent or I or the courts said didn't matter because she would live the way she wanted.

But history can repeat itself. I soon learned she had run from her father's house to Miami Bridge, a place for runaways, just as I had at almost the same age. She was going to Job Corps to finish high school. Life wasn't easy for her alone, but the medical research business gave us the ability to send extra money overseas to Danielle so she had some protection at least; she was not in danger of falling in with the wrong people out of necessity. She continued seeing my brother and his wife often enough.

Now came a most welcome reprieve from my lonely time in the countryside. Part of the pharmaceutical trial business was attending medical study conferences called investigator meetings. There we learned how to implement the protocols of each study we were doing at our hospital and heard about new breakthroughs and the results of previous studies. The conferences are held in major cities all over Europe, and Bobby decided to make another dream of mine come true: the dream of traveling to Italy, France, Germany, Greece, Austria, the Netherlands, England, and the Czech Republic, where we would go to meetings. It seems that marrying that sweet man in the Dominican Republic held no end of wonders and experiences. Every day I thanked God for this true deep blessing.

Not only was I able to see what a beautiful and unusual world this is, but I also was able to meet all kinds of different people. At the conferences we were introduced to many doctors and their wives from many different countries, and I was struck by the elegance and charm of so many different cultures. It seemed to me that Europeans were more sophisticated than Americans, and this brought out new insecurities in me. I knew what my life had been, and it looked very different from the lives of these educated, well-dressed people who appeared to have been on track all their lives. The women had a confidence and sense of style and femininity that made me feel diminished in some way. It was unlikely they had ever worked at a Hooters™, but we all know one shouldn't compare one's insides to someone's outsides. I was doing that very thing and, in my loneliness, and recent recovery from incipient drug addiction, I was finding myself wracked with low self-esteem around Bobby. Why would he want to be with a girl who had been homeless in Miami, a girl whose mother vilified her in the press? Why would anyone want to be? I had been used to pain all my life, and I now had found a new way to inflict it on myself. I started putting myself down incessantly.

Bobby had nothing to do with this negative internal voice of mine. He was always loving and totally involved with me. We were still in love, and we took many side trips to see these great historical capital cities where the conferences were held. For example, we toured Prague while we were there, experiencing its different architectures and beauty by the Brno River. Then, we took a train to elegant and aristocratic Vienna, with its musical and *fin de siècle* past. We toured London with its clock tower and St. Paul's; we took the tunnel to romantic, soft Paris with its beautiful buildings and special dazzling light. It was all magical, especially experiencing it with someone I deeply loved.

I have always been friendly, so everywhere we went we met interesting and free-spirited people. They did not seem to have suffered like I had, but seemed to know how to enjoy and trust life. So as happy as I was with Bobby and the world around me, I also felt as if I came up short in some way. I felt as if I did not have enough to offer. I also became jealous. *Shouldn't Bobby be with these people? They were so much better than me. They knew so much more. They were refined.* It was destructive thinking on my part and even I knew it. *Bobby loved me. Why was I torturing myself like this?* I am a person who, if I notice something I don't like about myself, changes, but I was also the kind of person who was drawn to pain and who did not mind hurting myself. After all, I was good at surviving pain, wasn't I? Didn't I show an aptitude for that?

I decided I would take this jealousy and really make myself confront it. I could be a cool wife like the other women who seemed so mature and open-minded. They all seemed to have affairs and be very avant-garde about sex. I would face my insecurity and be one of them. Our next trip was to beautiful Amsterdam. There, everyone smokes and drinks a lot and I was no stranger to that. I went along with it easily, and we were partaking daily. One evening over drinks, I suggested to Bobby, "Why don't we go to a strip joint and have some fun?" *Why should I be an American Puritan, a prude?* I thought. I can be as nonchalant as anyone else. "Come on," I said.

He thought it was a bit odd, but he likes to have a good time too, so off we went. There I saw the beautiful tall Dutch women with their perfect bodies (I had put on weight so my comparisons were painful, just like I wanted them to be). I told myself to have fun, be generous, do not focus on insecurities. *Any bad feelings I am having are growth experiences and they won't hurt me.* I remembered once dating a cop whom I made handcuff me when we got intimate so I could almost re-experience the pain of being raped. Deep inside me, I felt I deserved to be punished and to suffer. *That is who I am,* I told myself, *from the very beginning of life.*

In Europe, my main goal was to make Bobby happy and to be the most giving, open-minded, generous wife possible, so I came up with the idea of a threesome. *Isn't that generous of me?* I thought. *Aren't I the most blasé wife who gives her husband everything?* I told him that it would turn me on to see him with another woman. We would find a girl of my choosing in the red-light district. I would look for the prettiest one.

"Aimee, why would you want to do this?" he asked.

"So you don't feel deprived by being married; so you're not missing out."

"But it's not something that I want."

"Bobby, every man wants that. And I don't want to be with another man, so a threesome with two women is better. I just want you to be happy." He did not get that I was trying to hurt myself because this is not how a normal mind thinks, only one that grew up mixing love and hurt. He is also not one to stop anyone from being who they are.

"Are you sure about this?" he asked.

"Absolutely," I said, as I chugged back the strongest drink I could find. I was on a run. I set it up that we went to a brothel in Amsterdam where the girls were very young and attractive. I drank as much as I could to prepare myself to share the love of my life with another woman. I knew how forbidden sex was always more exciting, no matter who got hurt, so I was sure I was doing the right thing for Bobby. It wasn't about the swinging; it was about punishing myself, humiliating myself, and getting through it as I had as a child, although this time I had the drinks to anesthetize me.

We had the threesome and I survived it like I have survived other sex I did not want to have, and our marriage went on. We may not tell our grandkids, or maybe we will, although grandkids don't believe grandparents ever had sex. It just became another memory of how Bobby and I grew together. And probably as more time goes by, it will even become funny.

Soon Bobby said we had enough money to return home. The final push came when my sister said she would help out by buying us a car. We would continue the medical trials there, we decided. Bobby had made enough contacts around the world, and we could return to our former life and our former home. We could be back with Danielle, and I could be with my family. It had been two years since we'd left, and I missed my home, my sisters, my daughter, my miracle whip, and my peanut butter. I was ready to go home.

Chapter 21

Don't worry about anything, but pray about everything.
With thankful hearts offer up your prayers and requests to
God. Then, because you belong to Christ Jesus, God will
bless you with a peace that no one can completely
understand. And this peace will control the way you think
and feel.

Philippians 4:6-7

Our big house in Palmetto Bay was rented, so we moved into our duplex in Miami. It would take another year before we could move back into my dream house. Being in Miami, we were closer to Danielle, which had the benefit of making it easier for us to help her. Danielle turned out to be a hard worker and she lived on her own money doing different jobs, like waitressing, hostessing, and even as a recruiter, so we bought her a car to facilitate all her commuting. We all were happy to be back together, and Danielle would visit us every now and then, in spite of her busy social and work life. She was responsible, and she didn't smoke, do drugs, or drink, but I knew she had to have been affected by sixteen years of custody battles and all the changes I had gone through, not to mention her father's unkind temperament. It seemed that every time she had stayed with him, she couldn't wait to leave. I was happy to hear that when she turned eighteen, of her own will, she had resumed therapy with Dr. L-B.

When we got back, Bobby decided to open our own medical research business in a small office on "Calle 8." This business didn't last because we lacked the capital to pay for all the expenses while the business came in slowly, too slowly to meet all the bills. This is not uncommon for a start-up. Consequently, we partnered with Dr. Jeffrey Kamlet in Miami Beach. We would bring over the business, the equipment, and the patients in exchange for use of his office space for a 50/50 sharing of any profits. It seemed more than a fair offer to him. Yet it wasn't long before Dr. Jeffrey demanded more money. He insisted that Bobby not pay me for my work, although I had developed a strong knowledge base, having learned in Bulgaria and from all the conferences we had attended. Dr. Jeffrey believed my portion of pay should go to him; he considered Bobby and me as one person, which was ridiculous since I was putting in many hours processing and recording the data from the research studies. Dr. Jeffrey barely wanted to work but he wanted to increase his share of the profits.

We knew we had to leave; we were sure his demands would only keep increasing. We decided to start over again. This time, we would partner with two doctors in Homestead. Again, we brought in the business, the equipment, the employees, and the patients. These two doctors were thrilled, but once they saw the profits we could earn, they kicked us out and kept one of our best study coordinators, thinking they would go into competition with us. Whoever said partners ruin businesses wasn't wrong.

Then God's grace shone upon us once again. My sister Michelle came into a large amount of money she decided to share with us, giving us almost all of it so we would not need partners to survive. We would pay her back within five years. We started over again, but this time with our own capital in Palmetto Bay. All the employees with us in Homestead followed us, even Loyda, our longest, hardest working employee, even though, at first, she would have made more money if she had stayed in Homestead. Starting your own business is always challenging, but we now had the people, the clients, and the knowledge we needed to begin doing well. On top of that, I had family around me once again. I got to know my niece and nephews again, and our own kids got to know their cousins, aunts, and uncles, something I had always hoped for and wanted. I didn't want my own children to live through the family wars and secrets and nastiness that we had gone through as children. I didn't want them to suffer.

I was frustrated that Danielle had lived a lonely childhood while I struggled alone, without funds and family. I felt terrible about it and I spent a lot of time trying to make it up to her. But the other two were Bobby's kids and, this time, I could provide a stable background for them to thrive. Danielle even got to discover how having a nurturing father is healing for a child. Bobby helped her, was a friend to her, and let her know our home was always a home for her, too. The medical research center in Palmetto Bay kept doing better and better since we had earned a reputation in the medical study world during our time in Europe, and we had now been doing it for years. We had a great, loyal team, and although it included a diversity of backgrounds, political views, and lifestyles, there was harmony at work. Going to work was a pleasure for all of us. It wasn't that we didn't have our struggles since new businesses always take a while to be financially ahead of the game. Bobby was not only supporting all the employees but the five of us, as well as Danielle, who continually ran out of money, and we had to cover her bills. One funny thing that happened was that Dr. L-B had decided I was bipolar and had me on certain medications. Years later, I learned I am not bipolar at all, but I am not the first person to be misdiagnosed. Anyway, she then diagnosed her son as bipolar. She told me that he smoked like I do.

Somehow, since Latins see the world as one big family, I ended up inviting her son over when he got in touch with me, since he knew we were similarly diagnosed. I thought, *we can smoke, and I can learn more about this condition and even be there for him.* But it turned out that he would come over, pass out, or start crying, and I would think, *what did I get myself into?* His mother, my doctor, told me not to get too close to him but I was not scared of him. I knew, deep down, he was a sweet guy who was lost.

Bobby would sometimes come with me to see Dr. L.B. and he found it odd that I would not tell her very much. He would be the one who would inform her of what was going on with me. But she had lost my trust in the way she put down President Trump. That did not seem a necessary part of my therapeutic rehabilitation. We all know Trump polarized voters more than any other president than I can remember, but professionals manage to keep that out of their businesses. Bringing politics into treatment seemed a bit off course. *Which one of us*, I began to wonder, *needed therapy?*

So, in some ways I no longer had a therapeutic doctor. I was beginning to think these doctors were crazier than I was supposed to be. And was I even crazy? I had a stable life where I was able to be productive. Sure, I suffered from debilitating pain and depression at times, but I always came through on my work and family duties.

What was about to happen, though, would take every ounce of my strength, God's strength, and everyone's strength to get through. It was worse than anything that happened before. I was about to find out that I had to have that strength.

Chapter 22

Peace I leave with you; my peace I give you.
I do not give to you as the world gives. Do not let your hearts be
troubled and do not be afraid.
John 14-27

Danielle was my Valentine's baby who was born on February 13th. On her twenty-third birthday in 2016, we texted each other and I asked her if she would like to go out with us, but she had plans with a friend that night. We would celebrate over the weekend.

At this time, she was trying to become more independent, and she had put an ad on Craig's List for a roommate so she could live closer to downtown than where we lived. She interviewed a young man who claimed to be a health and fitness guru and a veteran. She agreed for him to move in but she felt that something was off about him. Instead of spending the first week there when he moved in, she went to spend a week with my brother Daniel and his wife Beatriz, with whom she was friends, despite my brother, Andres' son whom I had babied, liking to bad mouth me. Danielle was used to this from her father, and so she had learned to tune it out. Like other young people, she liked being part of a larger family. Maybe she also secretly liked having a black sheep mother, but after being there a week she decided to go to her own apartment and celebrate her birthday with a friend.

Byron Mitchell, her new roommate, was home, and the three of them shared a bottle of wine and were all together. On Valentine's Day, the day after her birthday, I got a call from Daniel's wife, Beatriz, that my first born, my sweet surprise, my docile but bold and strong girl was at Jackson Ryder Trauma Center fighting for her life.

"Get over there now," Beatriz said. "They are not telling me much, but they

118

are saying to get there fast."

Bobby and I rushed to the hospital, and when I got there, my sister Michelle and her family were there, too. Beatriz, Daniel, and I made sure to call everyone, and soon Brent and Candy came.

"Aimee," Beatriz said as I tore down the hall towards them, "They will not let us in, only you are allowed."

I entered with Bobby and the nurse said, "What you are about to see is very bad. The doctors do not have a good prognosis. She may not make it. She has been badly, badly beaten." I thought I was going to pass out when I saw her. Bobby held my arm.

Bobby and I went closer to the bed. There lay Danielle, in a coma, her neck twice its normal size and bruised as if someone had choked her. That's exactly what Byron had done so badly that she could not get any oxygen, which was one reason she had severe brain damage. Her face had been stitched from six very visible cuts that included both her eyelids and everywhere on her face. Her eyes were swollen shut with blood. Her head appeared to have been severely beaten too, with her hair all bloody. Her entire face was badly swollen because her nose, orbital bones, and mouth had been broken. There was no sign of life since she was not breathing on her own; she had immediately been placed on a respirator to breathe for her. Her Glasgow coma scale score was a three. On that scale from three to fifteen, three was the lowest possible score with a very low expectation of survival. She was practically dead, and the doctors were desperately sustaining her life. They transferred her from the emergency room to the trauma intensive care unit. I hugged Brent and Candy, choosing to forgive the past, and maybe in so much shock and terror that those two were the last thing on my mind. Everyone knows that there is nothing worse than losing a child.

The doctors and nurses were using cold packs to maintain her body temperature because it was out of control and she was constantly going into fevers because of the brain injury. Most of her injuries were in the head, with several fractures of the skull, including temporal bone, occipital bone, both orbital bones of the eyes, not to mention the broken nose, the broken mouth and teeth, with shoulder trauma and several brain hemorrhages. In all my rounds in a hospital, both as a kid and having worked in two emergency rooms I attended as a nursing student, I'd never seen such a horrible scenario. I couldn't believe it was my daughter, the one I had fought all my life to save from an abusive environment like I had lived in, only to find out that someone had now tried to kill her. I sat down and cried.

I wondered, *why hadn't I been there to stop it? Maybe I should have insisted that she live with us… if only she had asked us for money, so she didn't need a roommate.* I looked at this gentle girl, who was always considerate of others, who was the most excellent and patient sister in the world. She was mine in a different way than my other children. She and I had been alone, growing up together, suffering together, and growing strong together. I remembered her bringing me soup as a small child thinking it would make me feel better when I was depressed. She would be so happy when I worked in her schools on their school projects and was the cool mom. No matter how low I felt in my own life, I was always there. It was because of wanting to keep her that I finished school. It was because of her that I never let myself fall into drug addiction, and it was because of her that I would not die. I would not give up, no matter what I had gone through. I pushed myself in everything I did as a single mother, despite battling severe depression, because it was Danielle, not me, who was worth living for.

Strangely, as I sat in the chair crying, I didn't question God. I didn't ask why was I born only to suffer or why should my innocent child suffer? I didn't get mad at Him thinking He ignored the pact I made with Him: Let no one close to me die. I just thought that I must trust God and ultimately His will is perfect, that I will have to accept whatever the outcome. But I lowered my head to Him and prayed and prayed: Listen, God, I am willing to take whatever is left of her, even if she is a vegetable, so long as she doesn't die. I will feed her forever from a wheelchair through a tube in her stomach. Please don't let her die.

Bobby and I barraged the doctors for an accurate sense of what her true situation was. They explained, "This is touch and go. We don't know if she will live or die or even ever wake up."

While we all sat together and grieved, I learned the story: Danielle had been viciously attacked by the roommate (now in custody), who was an obvious monster and who had only been there a week. After the three people had shared a bottle of wine and Danielle's friend left, he had admitted the police that he had slammed her head against the tile floor several times and choked her for a long time. This is what was making it so difficult for her to wake up from the coma. We were to learn more about what had happened as the next few days unfolded.

When I got home, exhausted, I posted about what was going on on Facebook, asking for prayers. The response was tremendous. Even though I had been with Brent and Candy and Daniel and Beatriz, I did not feel their warmth or support. All the old mistrust was there, so I could not show my feelings. All of them had an attitude about me that was insulting and dismissive, but this was not the time to think about me. I kept to myself, and I was polite. I chose Facebook to reach out to a community, which may seem odd, but I was one of those people who had to rely on "the kindness of strangers," except for a few people in my family. And, indeed, I found a powerful community willing to pray and who recognized the horror we were going through. Many had experienced similar tragedies. They understood that all we could do now was trust God, the doctors, and the nurses and pray.

We were back the next day and every day after, while the doctors were doing daily MRIs and brain scans. After a week, her tests started to look better, and even though she was still unconscious, the doctors thought that in another week the swelling would go down and they would have a more accurate prognosis. They were now more hopeful she would live. She couldn't breathe on her own, but she did respond locally to acute pain at times. I began to learn more about the case. The police responded promptly to the 911 call with seventeen officers. Interestingly, Byron was the one who called 911 in the morning after the birthday party. The police had the attitude that it was just another domestic fight, but they arrived immediately, nonetheless. There were many of them and once they saw her, they knew this was not normal domestic violence. But they were not pressing charges.

Michelle, who had been a detective, informed me that the police had not done their job thoroughly and Danielle's hospital bed had not even been cleaned of her blood. Michelle knew the ropes and she started to get the police to pay attention, by badgering the police sergeant on duty. The police assigned an experienced homicide detective to handle the case, even though Danielle was not dead, but because there was a considerable chance of her dying.

In those twenty-four days, not knowing whether Danielle would live or die, I only stayed sane by thinking about what I could do to help her. It infuriated me that this murderer was not being treated as one. I went to the local TV channels to tell the story. I wanted to expose this monster and make the public aware of the dangers of moving in with a stranger. Danielle's story hit worldwide and tons of people from all over compassionately reached out to me with comforting words, some sharing their stories. This was wonderful, but more important, the outpouring of response and outrage shamed the police into going for the highest charge: a pre-meditated attempt at first-degree murder with a deadly weapon. This meant there was a possibility of getting the maximum sentence. I suppose I had learned something from my mother's old tricks of rallying the press. It had worked for her, and it was working for Danielle and me. Thirty-five-year-old Byron Mitchell was now locked up without bail. He told the police he had been in a relationship with Danielle, but this was not true; she hadn't even stayed at the apartment when he was there.

One person who contacted me through social media was a teacher who was also named Danielle, like my daughter. Not only did they have the same name, but they looked alike. Danielle Mars told me she lived in California where Byron Mitchell had once been a student before moving to Miami. He had apparently stalked Danielle Mars. He was so creepy, and it had scared her so much that she refused to teach a class he was taking. Danielle Mars heard about my Danielle's story and felt that she had dodged a bullet. The story even reached the news in England. With the internet, we can constantly reach people we do not know much about. We all take chances in this way and this story was showing how vulnerable we all are. None of us really knows who it may be that we are dealing with through the internet.

The doctors had now decided to cut a tracheostomy in Danielle's throat to connect the respirator machine after having placed a feeding tube in her stomach to give her liquid food. This was scary. But fourteen days later, Danielle was breathing on her own, assisted by the machine. The prayers were working. She had some eye movement but did not make eye contact or follow commands; she was still in the coma. I went home each night during those two weeks and prayed, and the number of other people praying on Facebook grew daily. I was interviewed again by several Miami TV channels who were now following the case. They asked what I was feeling. "It is in God's hands," I said.

Then I would go and sit with my daughter. She was still unconscious, and there was no guarantee she ever would be conscious again. Brent and Candy were also at the hospital every day. We took shifts caring for Danielle, although we barely spoke to each other. The hospital knew that Brent and I had a dual medical proxy for her. It had now been two weeks since the beating. Somehow, since the very start, I had remained strong; I couldn't lose myself for my family's sake, but in addition to the grief I was feeling for Dani, I had to see Brent and

Candy every day and they were always rude. I ignored it for my daughter's sake and to keep the peace. Beatriz and Daniel were also coming to visit, and it was the most miserable feeling to see they had allied with Brent, not their own blood. It seemed wrong, but I was used to it. I should have known that any civility among the family, Brent, and me could not last much longer.

Chapter 23

You, Lord, give perfect peace
To those who keep their purpose firm
And put their trust in you.
Trust in the Lord forever;
He will always protect us.
Isaiah 26:3-4

In March, two weeks later, Danielle's eyes began following the nurse, but she was not yet out of the coma. When her eyes opened slightly, all you could see was blood —no irises or pupils. I was terrified. The doctors and nurses said it was normal because of the trauma. At that point, it was still very difficult to maintain her body temperature. For me, watching her there, without moving, was agonizing. *Would she return to herself? Would she ever come back?* All we could see was a slight agitation, probably her wounds itching and hurting. She didn't sleep at night because of the pain, so she often slept during the day. She had now started looking at me, but she was not seeing anything. I would put my arms around her and just hold her.

After a long twenty-four days, I was sitting with Danielle, when I heard, faintly, "Mom?"

I jumped up. "Dani, Dani, I love you. You are okay, you are safe now."

"I am?"

"Yes, you are healing. You will be perfect soon."

"I will?"

"Yes, yes," I said smiling, gently stroking her hair, and holding her. She had spoken!

All night I kept saying to Bobby, "She spoke!" I reported it on Facebook and fireworks and applause and hallelujah emoticons inundated my page. I went back to the hospital the next day feeling excited. What did she want? What did she need? What could I do for her? I had a thousand questions. But she was back in the coma and unresponsive. The previous day had been a freak incident. Apparently, this can happen to people in comas. Now she lay still. Brent and Candy were also visiting daily, and we would politely leave each other time with Danielle in private. The next day when Bobby and I came in, we overheard (keep in mind Bobby and I are both in the medical field) that Brent had ordered that the doctors take Danielle off two medications. One of these medicines was for pain, but Brent stated that it was slowing her ability to wake up. Brent is not a doctor; he had no right to order nurses to do this.

We immediately went into Danielle's room and saw she was biting her hand and pulling her hair, which are known signs of intense pain. We rushed out to Brent and Candy, asking, "Do you have any idea how she must be hurting?" They turned away, refusing to even speak to us.

Candy said, "This is the right decision."

We were shocked at their cruelty, leaving her there squirming in pain. We decided to file for guardianship so there would be a process for how the two couples would negotiate the upcoming decisions. Brent and Candy were back to their old tricks of making unilateral decisions, and their old tricks had never considered what was right for the child. They had begun having meetings with doctors without us and acting as if they were the sole guardians.

The next day we came to visit, and the guard said, "You are not allowed to enter." We looked down at the paper and saw that Danielle was now listed as a security patient. We went to guest services and were able to add our name to the visitor list, once we pointed out that I was a proxy too. It wasn't very difficult to figure out who had taken our names off the list.

We continued the process of filing for guardianship because we were getting frightened that Brent's cruelty could have terribly detrimental effects on Danielle's health. Meanwhile, the doctor suggested that we take turns staying with her at night, which we did. But her caretakers were back at war, which was a terrible situation for the child and for everyone else involved. Brent had also gone to court, and the judge could see there was no way for us to reconcile, so he asked if we would agree to a court-appointed guardian who would overlook the medication and the decisions being made for Danielle. Out of desperation and not wanting Brent to have any power, we agreed.

We went to the hospital on day twenty-eight of this ordeal. I went with a heavy heart; it was so painful to see my daughter lying there like that, but this time… she was awake! She had come out of it. I hugged her and cried, Bobby cried with us, and never had there been a sweeter day. She was getting better, and they were going to let her start breathing without the tracheostomy. It was official. She was out of the coma.

Every channel was covering this case, Channels 4, 7, 10, 23, 51, and 24, and they were interviewing me almost daily. I got a lot of comfort from knowing that by creating awareness they were exposing the terrible person who had perpetrated this crime while possibly saving the next person who took in an unknown roommate. Through my interviews, I began developing friendships with the news anchors. They seemed to genuinely care; many of them were family people themselves, and there was a great positive response from the Miami and national communities. What Danielle had gone through was every parent's worst nightmare. Now I could tell the media, and everyone, that she was out of the coma. She would live! It felt like everyone was rooting for her. It meant a lot to me.

I especially developed a friendship with Michael Siden from Channel 10, who keeps in touch to this day. He was an intelligent, handsome anchor, and he gave our family caring support which we truly appreciated. Danielle was now on the step-down trauma floor where she would have therapy twice a day. Brent and Candy were still visiting daily, as were Bobby and I, so I decided to avoid them and went to visit when they said they would not be there on Tuesday and Thursday mornings. We came, as planned, only to find out that Brent wanted to move her to Broward, to another facility, but he had never told us. They stayed in the room during my visiting time, and when Dani tried to hug me, Candy rushed over and got in the way to stop it. This was my daughter.

"We've decided not to leave you alone with Dani," they said.

I wanted to punch her, but that is not my way. Then, the guardian, Anita Kimler, came in. She knew what was going on and made notes. "I will come back with a plan very soon," she said. And she seemed to be the type of person who would. At this point, I was almost high from Dani being out of the coma. That was what was important. I did not feel safe expressing any feelings in the hospital; I only talked openly with Dani and Bobby. When I would get home after seeing her, I would write on Facebook: "She is out of the coma, officially." "I believe in miracles." "I love you princess." "Danielle is a fighter."

Again, there were so many responses of love and support. It was wonderful, but of course, I was sad that this response had to come from strangers. This had been my life. I went back on my visitation schedule, and I knew Michelle wanted to see Danielle, so she came with me. We got there and Brent and Candy wouldn't let Michelle in, either. Daniel and Beatriz were also there, and as I went to say hello to my daughter, Beatriz screamed out in front of Danielle, as she lay there, "Your mother is a bitch. Everyone knows it. She is only out for herself."

A hoarse, weak little voice from the bed spoke, saying, "No, she isn't."

Then my brother Daniel turned to Dani and said, "You are as crazy as she is if you believe that. You two are no good."

Brent said, "Aimee is the one who is no good. Everyone knows that."

Bobby tore out of the room to tell the guardian how these people were behaving, "Not only is it all lies, but this is terrible for Dani's health to live through this kind of ugliness." The guardian agreed with him. She came in and asked Brent to leave. He didn't. I knew that it was war. Bobby and I were expecting more trouble, and we just hoped Anita Kimler could handle it. Meanwhile, we focused on Dani. At the new neurorehabilitation floor, she began getting physical therapy five times a day. Now she was eating soft food. Soon it would be normal food. She was making visible progress every day. But her father's behavior was not improving, and his behavior was endangering her. "You know," he said to her, "Your mother does not care about you."

Dani was used to this and perhaps she closed her mind to the negativity. But then they told her, "Your mom has hired a better attorney for the attacker so that he can get out of jail." Dani probably knew this was impossible, but this kind of hatred and having to even entertain this kind of thought was not good for her recovery. She began getting upset, crying, and she lost her appetite. I do not know what Daniel and Beatriz were saying but, for her, in this state, to hear these continual vitriolic put-downs of her mother had to be horrible. She was not able to counter them, nor should she have had to.

That night she sent her father a text, "Please do not come. I do not want to see adults." Brent now began posting terrible things about me on Facebook and the guardian, Anita, saw this. It infuriated her and she took away everyone's visiting rights when she figured out what was going on. Anita had decided to only allow Daniel and Beatriz visitation rights since she thought they were neutral while she figured out what to do about the fighting parents. She did not know that Beatriz and Daniel were also saying negative things about me to my daughter. Beatriz would post on Facebook that I had contacted the press for my own gain. She told Dani the same and that I had tried to take her out of the hospital while she was still tied to a tracheostomy. These were all outright lies and terrible for Dani's soul. Later, I would find out why these two were out to punish me. Only a guilty person loves to accuse with this much vengeance. The worst part was that I was not allowed to see Dani because of Brent's tricks and madness. The guardian took away Dani's phone. "I am doing this," Ms. Kimler said, "so there is less emotional pressure on Danielle."

Dani and I had spoken every day while she was in therapy, so I had an idea of what was going on and I could give her love. Not having contact with Danielle was another horrible loss.

However, soon this guardian was to do what so many of my lawyers had done with the unending hatred around us. She resigned. The family was too toxic. We were now going to be assigned to a new guardian from the Guardianship Program of Dade County, but the one who had been assigned took his time to show up. That person would eventually allow me to see Dani and get things back to normal, but we were not allowed to begin until someone took over the case. Bobby tried to email them and call them, but they never answered. He even went to the guardianship office, where he was thrown out by one of the people there who knew about the case, saying that he was very busy and that he has to investigate, and he would call us.

We called Anita Kimler and she also said she tried to call them, to no avail. Anita was sorry about the situation; this had never been her intention. I was still not allowed to see Dani, and now this situation amounted to twenty days where I had not seen her or known anything about her, which is a very long time for a severely ill child. I knew she was going through the arduous process of learning to eat and walk again, but I was not allowed to be there to help her. The new guardian was doing nothing; he had not even appeared. It was a kind of hell to be stopped from seeing my daughter just when she needed me most. Danielle found a way to call me from her hospital bed, but soon they took the room phone also. The cruelest thing you can do to a child is to take away her mother.

It seemed insane that she had endured everything, and she was now being punished by not being allowed a support system. Bobby tried to resolve it through all the channels of the hospital, but to no avail.

I felt like I was being torn apart inside. Jennifer helped Danielle

get an attorney to defend her rights, but the attorney was denied by the guardianship program and the hospital. Danielle called the attorney anyway, but when he visited her in the hospital, he was kicked out by security. Even convicted criminals have the right to counsel. Besides Brent and my own family not communicating with me, I was well-aware that I never heard from my mother throughout Danielle's hospitalization. Little Sean, my twelve-year-old son, would ask about his grandmother. "Where is she?"

I said, "She is not interested in us."

With his sweet nature, he suggested we send her an edible arrangement. He said that he knew it would not change things, but he wanted me to send it anonymously to be kind, regardless. I smiled at his optimism, but I knew nothing could change things if my mother was still this silent and uncaring after all these years. She had to have known what was going on through her son Daniel. Even though I was used to this treatment, it was difficult to feel that everything around me was inhuman. The only things that provided light to me were Bobby, my own children, and my love for Danielle. I was forbidden to see her, but I knew that she would feel my love through the airwaves. She knew I had never let her go, no matter what. I decided to only focus on that.

Chapter 24

But the righteous are glad and rejoice in his presence;
They are happy and shout for joy.
Sing to God, sing praises to his name;
Prepare a way for him who rides on the clouds.
His name is the Lord – be glad in his presence!
Psalm 68:3-4

After being separated from my daughter for twenty days, we were told we could start visiting Danielle for two hours every other day. I was so excited. I wanted to see how she had improved. As we rushed down the hallway to her room, the new guardian, Raymond Hardy, was leaving her room. Bobby stopped him as he came down the hall and asked, "Can you tell us what the next steps are?" (A typical Bobby question).

"I haven't decided," the guardian answered. Bobby felt a wave of frustration and then Hardy said, "And please keep in mind what will happen will be my, and only my decision." Once we got to the nurses' station, we were told that we had to turn in our cell phones before seeing Danielle. I wasn't quite sure why, but I didn't care —I would have turned over our entire bank account to see her. When we opened the door (which we were not allowed to close during our visit), I saw she was thinner. She had lost ten pounds, we found out, but we were so happy to just talk and hug and to see that she was indeed making remarkable improvements. Danielle was now feeding herself and slowly walking. The swelling in her face had gone down and she looked beautiful. She told us that she was not allowed outside or to have devices. Only family members could see her now.

"I see on the board in your room," I said, "that you will be released in two days."

"Yes," she smiled. "I can't wait to go home with you." This was all a dream come true for Bobby and me. Danielle was well, functioning a bit more slowly mentally and physically than she used to, but she was not dead or brain damaged. She would soon be home with us where I knew we would take good care of her.

"You have no idea," I said, "how many Facebook wishes you received for your good health. Literally, thousands of people have been praying for you. You are really loved." Then I read her some of the postings.

I said, "And you have been on the news almost every day. Everyone has been rooting for you and thinking about you."

"Daniel thinks you are on the news for your own gain..." she said.

"Of course, he does," I laughed, "but the reason I went to the press is to raise awareness about what this monster did to you. I want them to know so they can put him away for good." Danielle nodded, and we talked of other things: how she felt, what the doctors and nurses were like, crazy things her sister Michelle had said, what was going on with her pets at my house, and what she needed now.

Too quickly, our two hours were over, and she said in her normal voice, "Mom, I wish you could stay longer." Her normal voice! God was undoubtedly good. When we left her room, we went to see her doctor, Dr. Alvarez, who confirmed that there were no medical issues requiring her to stay in the hospital and, yes, she would be allowed to leave in a few days, but she would need to be monitored. We agreed completely and were looking forward to it. As scheduled, she was cleared to leave the hospital for outpatient treatment, but she could not leave without the sign off from her guardian. She was so anxious as she waited (unbelievably, he did not come for four days). Danielle very much wanted to go outside. I wheeled her out to an open patio where she drank in the sun and flowers and palm trees. The outside world was waiting for her.

Thanks to this "guardian," Danielle ended up being in the hospital for twenty extra days because the hospital didn't know whom to discharge her to. Daniel and Beatriz had their own visitation times with Danielle, as did Brent and Candy. Bobby and I had to see her on separate days because Daniel and Beatriz had teamed up with Brent and Candy and they were painting a very dark picture of us to the hospital staff. But worse, they were still trying to denigrate me to a gullible, recovering Danielle. Brent would not let up about me, yelling, "Your mother is a piece of shit. You know what? I am getting custody so I can put you in a facility for treatment. You are not ready to be let out. You cannot go to your mother."

Even though I felt I could take the best care of Danielle, I could clearly see that she was tired of being in the hospital and I had decided to support wherever she was going to go, except Brent's. Daniel and Beatriz claimed that Danielle would be better off with them because she had stayed with them the week leading up to the incident. "And anyway," they said to Danielle, "it is better for you than staying with such a horrible mother, one who wrongfully accused her father of sexual abuse." They must have also been telling the guardian this.

Brent and Candy apparently corroborated this story since, unbelievably, they were friends with my mother. According to them, I had made up the story of Andres abusing me. It seemed "The Case from Hell" was still in play as a mud-slinging tool for the family. I focused my energy on Danielle being in the hospital so long and wanting to get out. But these two couples had done their damage with the guardian, and I was now no longer allowed to spend the night with her. The guardian then decided that Daniel and Beatriz were the only ones who could see her any time they wanted. Danielle may have been making progress, but she was still ill. Not knowing how she was faring made me sick to my stomach, but I had no choice but to ignore it. I couldn't show weakness or my own family would fall apart, so I took to Facebook, writing everything down and relying on the kind responses of strangers. These responses were therapeutic. We needed each other.

Finally, the guardian let us see Danielle again for two hours every other day. For Danielle to get discharged, he required that I agree that she be released to Daniel and Beatriz. He felt (and in this he was right) that her going there would avoid yet another custody battle. She went home with them. We would talk on the phone, and I could hear that she was unhappy. I was not surprised after one week with them that I got a call from Danielle asking if she could stay with us.

"Of course. What happened?" I asked. She went on to explain that Beatriz had thrown all her clothes out on the lawn in the rain and had essentially thrown her out. This was a girl who was still traumatized and needed stability to heal.

"Why?" I asked, adding, "Tell me later." I knew it would only be some vindictive, made-up tale. How these people loved drama and a scapegoat. We immediately went to get her, and she was reunited with her own room, her pet, her family, and a feeling of safety. I could almost see the relief on her face as she padded around her old home in her pink pajamas. Danielle later told me what had happened with Beatriz and Daniel. Apparently, Brent's large family was having a gathering and Danielle told Candy that she did not want to go if Daniel and Beatriz were coming, even though she was staying with them. Would Candy please un-invite them?

Candy asked, "Why are you saying that? I thought you liked being with them." Candy expressed shock and then Danielle went explained, "I never told any of you, but Daniel molested me once while I was half asleep when I was sixteen. I froze as it was happening, but now I can't forget it."

Candy said, "Does anyone else know?"

"I told Henry, Sabrina, and Rey years ago and they remember. You can ask them if you want."

Candy immediately told Danielle's father, Brent, who in turn, called Daniel because Brent could not believe such a thing was true. He was friends with Daniel and thought the brain damage was affecting his daughter. Never did it occur to him that Danielle might be telling the truth. Brent was too affected by my mother and her stories. Brent sent Danielle many text messages, questioning her and accusing her of lying. Danielle, taking after her mother, decided to tape record her ex-boyfriend Ray affirming that she had told him about it at the time. She used the same tactic I did since, like me, one of her parents did not believe her. I was shocked by the way history was repeating itself, but after everything I had been through, it was not hard for me to imagine that Andres' son would mimic his father's behavior, just like my daughter had often repeated my own behavior.

The important thing was that Danielle was finally at home with us, where she should have been all along. But this business with my brother Daniel deeply bothered me. After a few days, I asked her more about what had happened at Daniel's when she was staying there after her release from the hospital.

"I hate how everyone talks about you and Bobby. I missed the kids too," she said.

"Why did you never tell me before about Daniel's behavior when you were a teenager?" I asked.

She and I were sitting near the kitchen. "Well…" she said slowly, her head hanging, "I didn't want to upset everyone. There was always so much fighting in our family." She was right about that. I sat there and vaped on my electronic cigarette. The fact was that now I understood why Daniel was so hateful to me in front of her. He thought he could keep her silent by maligning me. He was telling her in code that if she talked, she too would be maligned. Plus, he wanted to feel better than me, all the while knowing that he wasn't. It was easier for him to focus on me being a villain than to look at himself. He also probably thought that if she did talk, it would be easy to call her a liar with her having a severe brain injury and a mother with zero credibility, if not for the tape recordings of Andres. Luckily, though, Danielle had not only told her boyfriend,

But also two of her friends when she was sixteen.

Even though some of these friends did not want to be involved in any litigation or problems, I was impressed by how clever my daughter had been. Most important, I now knew she would stay away from these despicable people. Like father, like son. While she was recovering with us, Brent had started yet another legal proceeding for custody of Danielle as an adult. In and of itself that was crazy. Of course, I don't know why I was surprised by this. Brent and Candy just loved to sue. They had sued Brent's brother for custody of his daughter, I found out from Danielle, and they had even won. Like Danielle, this girl ran away from them, too when she was sixteen. They were suing Honda at the time, for God knows what. But it took three attorneys this time and the great grace of God to keep Danielle with us and make the unnecessary proceedings go away. Besides, I had a good idea the judge was no dummy.

During the hearing, he looked down his glasses at Brent's team and said, "This young woman Danielle can talk, thank you, and she wants to live with her mother, not in a facility. She is not a minor and," he stood up, "case closed." The case that should have been opened was the one involving Byron Mitchell. In August, they were supposed to go to court, but his lawyers kept resigning on him. They were not ready to go to court. Years later, as I write this, they are still not ready. The case has yet to go to trial.

Today, Danielle, who used to have twenty-twenty vision, needs glasses. Our dentist, when he heard about Danielle's broken front teeth, gave us his cell number and fixed her up for free, a true act of kindness. Dr. John Addison, this gentle and good man, has been our dentist ever since. There have been many acts of compassion and love coming toward her from every side: from doctors, Jennifer, friends, and people everywhere. Now, Danielle walks a little differently and she can no longer ride a bike. Otherwise, she is Danielle, and she has healed better than I expected. This whole situation has been a great lesson. What is the lesson? To trust God and to love your child with unconditional love as she makes a slow, but blessed recovery. That love is the healing agent.

Chapter 25

Heavenly Father, I come to you with a broken and shattered heart.
The Scripture says that a broken and contrite heart will you not
despise, I ask that you will give me the grace to overcome the
temptations of adultery in Jesus' name. **based on Psalm 147:3**

Michelle, my youngest daughter, is growing up and walks around hugging her shih tzu puppies, Peanut and Gizmo. My ten-year-old daughter gives me advice on life and tells me involved stories about her friends at school. She has a beautiful singing voice, as did my mother. This little daughter is growing up big in personality and inner and outer beauty. I often find myself transfixed by her and she reminds me of parts of myself, if I had not been wounded as I was.

Sean is handsome and smart and likes to be funny like his father. He has a heart as wide as the sea, like both his parents. He is a teenager, so he is a mystery man, but I do not worry about him since I know he is balanced. It is clear to me he will go far in life, like his father. His father, unlike Andres, is a genius in his work and Sean has inherited all those qualities.

Danielle, my big little girl, now works with us, has a room here and sleeps in her own place. She is getting better slowly and often has outbursts of frustration. Sometimes, both she and I have to access our inner peacefulness when dealing with each other. We get through it, as mothers and daughters do. We know that we are each other's first loves.

My mother and father and many of my siblings remain uninterested in my life and unkind when they speak of me. Even so, I pray for my mother daily. Beatriz ran into Danielle at a big box store and yelled out to Danielle, "Who are you whoring with now? Who is your mother whoring with, too? Like mother, like daughter." Danielle defended herself and Beatriz punched her, even knowing that my daughter had just suffered a severe brain trauma.

Danielle took out a year-long restraining order on Beatriz, and well she should have. I don't know why I was born to these angry and bitter people, but so be it.

I also know I was born to a loving God. My nature is to see the good in people and not to overreact to terrible behavior. I was able to see my way through.

I kept getting better daily. It started with saying the rosary every day, sometimes even twice. This ritual balanced and settled my soul. It is a form of meditation, and it has magical effects. It solidified for me that love is the only answer, as the song goes, and when I find loving solutions to our problems, I know they are the right ones. The rosary also gives me hope. I came up with the idea of writing this book while praying the rosary. The rosary has made me feel that I am not alone and that I can recite these prayers to Mary for the saving of sinners. I have known many sinners, and like all of us, have been one myself.

After working hard on writing this book, we finally launched the first edition. We won five awards for it and I started a talk radio program, "The Cure," which is now nationally syndicated through Total Truth Network/ Salem Radio, Sirius XM 131 Family Talk. People call in with what they are going through and I am starting to get quite a following. The shows focus on themes such as God's will and helpful hints on how to pray. Almost a million people are interacting with me on Facebook, many saying I am helping them. I am realizing my purpose in God's direction for me.

But as happy as I was and thriving, it turned out the devil wasn't through with me yet. Bobby and I were in our twentieth year of marriage, and I could not have been more happy with him. But there were still lessons to learn.

One Sunday afternoon, Bobby, Jennifer and I and a whole lot of other friends went boating, as we often did, and Jennifer was drinking a lot, as she sometimes does. Bobby and I don't drink anymore. I was used to her being drunk; sometimes she would come over to the house high, and I just accepted it as part of Jennifer. When she was sober, she was responsible and a good friend, but drunk, Jennifer could be crazy. But who am I to judge anyone?

But that day on the boat, I saw she was drunk, and I watched her go over to my husband, get between his legs and say to me, "I am rubbing your husband's dick and balls." I was more than aware Jennifer's drunken behavior could get unpredictable, but I froze. For some reason, I then did what I always do in extreme pain, I pretended it wasn't bothering me. I trusted Bobby but could not help but notice that he was smiling and had his arms around Jennifer and allowing her to stay between his legs for several pictures that our friend Paola was taking of them, as well as of everyone else.

I went to another part of the boat and turned away. It sickened me and I didn't want to be part of it. Nothing is worse than someone sober having to interact with someone drunk. I didn't know how Bobby could take it.

I suddenly remembered another time I had turned away from what she was doing. Four years earlier, we had all gone to a club together and were partying. At that time Bobby and I were drinking, and she did a lap dance for Bobby. I got angry at the time and confronted her the next morning. She claimed she didn't remember doing it. I asked him about it and he claimed he didn't remember her doing it, but I remembered. She became furious that I accused her and quit working for us.

Eventually she returned to her job and I decided to forgive them. They both seemed to have no memory of it; they were drunk, and people behave badly when they're drunk. God knows I had done so, and I put it out of my mind. Until that Sunday on the boat. This was a bit too much of a recurrence.

After we dropped Jennifer off after the boat ride, I asked Bobby, "How is it that Jennifer only gets sexual like that with you?"

"Oh, come on. That's how she is with everyone."

Something didn't sit right.

We got home and Paola sent all the afternoon pictures to us. In every picture, Jennifer was all over Bobby and no one else.

The next morning when I opened my Facebook page there was a picture Jennifer posted of herself hugging Bobby with her chest pressed against him and his arms around her.

This was the only picture Bobby and I had not received from Paola. Besides feeling disrespected by both Jennifer and Bobby, I asked myself, "Is this a good way for me, who has a religious program and is on social media where people call me 'the minister,' to show my family life?" These pictures were inappropriate and misleading.

And then I began to wonder what was going on here. Now I allowed my feelings of vulnerability, betrayal and hurt to come crashing down on me, *my beloved husband and best friend acting so sexual right in front of me, knowing it would be agony for me.* I desperately needed God's help during this.

I began expressing to Bobby how hurt I was about what happened on the boat. I said, "It makes me feel unloved and you're not taking our marriage seriously. It's not the right way to behave."

"You know Jennifer is crazy," he replied, not taking any responsibility for the fact he did not push her away himself.

"And what about that lap dance four years ago?"

"What lap dance? You must be thinking of someone else. I don't remember."

His denial started to remind me too much of my childhood. "Bobby, you have to take some responsibility here. "

It broke my heart that he wouldn't admit he did something wrong. It was déjà vu of having to suffer through people behaving sexually and acting like it wasn't happening. No way was I going to live through that again. Absolutely not. And what really WAS going on?

We went at it for seven days. "What do you want from me?" he shouted.

"I would have liked you to push her away on the boat and show integrity and devotion for our marriage, after 20 years of marriage where our love has grown stronger, and we have gotten closer to God. That's what I want from you. Do you know how hurt I am that you don't seem to love me enough to do the right thing or even recognize that it was wrong? You don't even acknowledge what happened four years ago. What else are you not acknowledging?"

I spoke to Jennifer, and she did say she was sorry and that she was wrong about what happened on the boat, but Bobby was adamant about not remembering years back and he minimized the boat incident as Jennifer being Jennifer and not recalling the details as I did.

My problem now became, *who is Bobby? Is my saint really a passive player in what the devil gets up to?*

I called Jennifer to ask her to confirm that the recent boat incident happened since Bobby would not. But then Jennifer switched her story, doubled down, accused me of false allegations and quit working with us again.

Suddenly I felt totally negated; Bobby claimed I was having a false memory. Here I was, finding myself in this position where my best friend and my husband have betrayed me in countless ways for the second time and now Bobby is stonewalling me.

After I cried for seven days and threatened to leave him, Bobby still couldn't remember anything or acknowledge his part.

On the seventh day, I was beside myself. My own husband was trying to pawn off his irresponsible behavior as imaginary.

We were in our bedroom. "Bobby, if you don't tell me the truth, I will kill myself. Our marriage has been based on the truth. I grew up around horrendous lies. If you think I want to continue a life of living more of them, you are wrong. I am out of here. I am going to God directly, all of me. Be honest about what happened with Jennifer. I never thought you could lie to me. Now we need to start being honest with each other about everything, starting with the affair in the Dominican Republic. If you are lying to me now, you must have lied to me in the past and I need to know that you can be honest. If we continue this marriage, you need to start telling me the truth. If you won't, then this relationship will go nowhere. What is the point?"

He decided to tell me the truth.

He turned to me and said, "Yes Jennifer gave me a lap dance."

This was not a tremendous shock to me, but at least he was admitting it now.

"What about the truth of what happened in the Dominican Republic when I met you? Tell me everything. Our marriage won't work unless there is trust and we are honest with each other."

"I've told you, she just went down on me but we didn't have sex because she was a virgin."

I still didn't believe him, even though he repeated it to the marriage counselor. By the grace of God, who gave me the right words at that moment, I said, "You claim to love me, but doing what you want seems more important than making things right, by being fully honest."

So, he confessed that it was a real affair in the Dominican Republic. I knew it anyway in my heart.

Now, because he did tell me the truth, we could heal. To realize he could lie to me and had been lying to me our entire marriage was a hard pill to swallow. Now it was up to me and God. I was faced with the choice of having blind faith, not in him but in God. There is no guarantee that Bobby will do the right thing, should he be faced with the same situation again, but if I trust in God, I will have strength to handle whatever happens.

And I can help Bobby by dissociating ourselves from my past friends who are still living a much different lifestyle. It's time to let go of the idea that I am loyal no matter how a friend like Jennifer behaves, and to console myself by taking pride in having a friend for over 25 years. I remember that it was said, "If your right hand causes you to sin, cut it off." I can still love those friends in prayer.

But I chose to love Bobby unconditionally. I know the good in him outweighs the bad and I don't believe he ever meant to hurt me. I do believe people can change if they want it badly enough, even after 20 years of a successful marriage. Not all fairy tales or romantic love stories are perfect and even heroes have wounds. This experience made me realize that all I need is God, and no matter how difficult, there are battles worth fighting and people that I will never give up on.

Bobby is one of them. If he isn't, God can make him the husband that he needs to be.

And that's exactly what happened next.

God made him the husband that he and I needed him to be.

And, as if God was sending me a message, the Jesuit priest from the church where we got married told us about the DVD, *Freedom through Christ*, and, as I watched, the words rang out to me: "The bigger the offense, and the more just the claim, the more important it is to forgive and the more merit it has. Think about Jesus."

That became my strategy and lesson. I remembered that the enemy wants to destroy sacred unities and exceptional love anointed by God. I would not help the enemy. Bobby and I began devising a way back to each other. Not surprisingly, it was with the help of God.

Chapter 26

Prayer for happiness
Father,
Please help me to rest in your happiness,
To allow a smile to linger on my lips,
To dwell within a wonderful memory,
To walk back through sunlit places.
Please help me to awake with hope,
To engage with life in all its variety,
To take in the beauty of others' joys,
To touch the souls of those I meet with thankfulness.
Please help me to sing with faith,
To carry the truth close in my heart always,
To rejoice at new life and
To have peace as I age.
Please help me to indulge in love
To breathe in the sweetness of intimacy,
To taste the kindness of friendship,
To feel the warmth of embrace.
Please help me not to miss
A single drop of heaven,
To catch each moment
And drink the great joy of life.
Amen. **Unknown**

First, I knew deep in my heart that I could not give up on Bobby. After all, think of how he had never given up on me – when I went on crack, when we had to fight custody battles, and when I was depressed and didn't want to live. I had once seen a quote to the effect that "the perfect marriage are two imperfect people who refuse to give up on each other." How could I now turn on the one person who had stood beside me through all my own imperfections?

Am I to sit in judgement of others when they fall?

Bobby is a good person. He had just been tempted, as we all can be. Part of our prayers say, "Deliver us from evil," since we are twenty-four/seven being tempted. Most of us think we're smarter than the devil, but if we are honest with ourselves, we're not. That is why we have no right to just look at the surface of our own and others' mistakes and pass judgment or run away from each other. Those mistakes most often lead us to a deeper healing.

That is exactly what happened with Bobby and me.

I have always prayed rosaries, as you know, and I believe the demons felt threatened when the prayers increased. So, they came out with a vengeance and that was how the boat incident happened and Bobby's denial. We had even considered divorcing because while I cried in grief and even prayed through the tears, anger, and the pain, slowly I was giving up hope on life.

But now I began praying 30 rosaries most days -- The Joyful, Sorrowful, Luminous, and Glorious Mysteries, and this dedication to prayer changed both of us. Amazingly, Bobby began praying with me. That was a big change, since he had never behaved like that. Furthermore, we started confessing every time as we attended mass weekly.

We both got up at 3:00 in the morning, like monks do, and started our prayer day. He read the Bible the first 30 minutes followed by a 30-minute rosary with me. We finished at 4:30 am. I swept and mopped as I said my rosaries throughout two hours of fastidious cleaning; he did the same as we said them, then he went to work. I woke up the kids and got them ready for school, then continued my duties and praying until meeting Bobby for lunch. Later in the day, from 4 to 5 at night, I prayed my last rosaries alone as I swept our house a second time. I discovered this is what worked best for my peace of mind.

What caused us to intensify our prayer life like this and thus heal?

The Jesuit priest in the church I attended invited us to a general confession, which is a transformational act and reveals new horizons in the spiritual world. It turned out it was not only Bobby who needed to release demons, but me too. The priest told me I had to quit smoking and vaping if I wanted to make spiritual progress. This was enormous to me. He also said I was being called to be a saint (he feels this about many of us) but I had noticed that when I prayed for someone, results happened. So, I listened attentively about this calling.

But I didn't think I could live without vaping and weed, and I told the priest so.

"Do it today," he said. "There is no time. God will give you the grace."

I thought, *well, let's see, let's see if He gives me the grace.*

I went home and did it. I went cold turkey. I sold the weed back to the seller, as well as all the paraphernalia. I could not believe it. I was able to maintain abstinence.

I told the priest about it a week later as I was leaving the confessional.

He yelled, "God is forming you into a saint." I slammed the door behind me I was so nervous.

So, you see, I too changed as Bobby was doing with his reading of the Bible and praying rosaries. For example, he realized he shouldn't be negative or in denial and as he did so, he became more open, more vulnerable, and humbler.

Another effect I felt was my depression lifting, as the only stimulant we now were using was prayer. I felt better and better about our lives and was clear that I could not possibly live without God and without Bobby.

I also learned more about the roads that can let the devil in. I did not know, for instance, that gossiping is a sin because we are passing judgment about matters we do not know about. Curiosity is a sin, because we can be curious about what is wrong in life, which gives the enemy more power to sneak into our lives.

The priest was right: I did not need medicine, dope, vaping or drinking. In other words, if you stay close to God, you have self-control and you need nothing but Him.

I have always been a person who likes to do things correctly, who doesn't procrastinate. I think if we are sinning or doing things without full attention and without honoring giving the best of ourselves to whatever we do, it is an insult to the soul.

This new lifestyle made my life and relationship with Bobby better than ever. If I thought it was good before, I didn't know what good was.

The priest said to me, "God is calling you to be a saint. God can show you so much more than you already know."

Funnily enough, I began doing something I never thought I would ever do. A new door in me opened. I began writing poems about God to current pop songs. I would read them on my radio show and people loved them.

I also saw that I was better at relationships and more loving with Bobby, of course, but also with my kids, our dogs, those we know, and those we encounter. I appreciate nature more, and little things made me happier than ever.

I need to pray at least 28 rosaries daily, which equates to seven crowns. According to Saint Louis de Monfort and expressed by Saint Juan Diego in his vision of the Lady of Guadalupe, every time we say the rosary devoutly, crowns of 150 red roses and 16 white roses are placed upon the heads of Jesus and Mary that are heavenly, never fade, nor ever lose their exquisite beauty. For me, this crown was completed every 4 rosaries, representing the Joyful, Luminous, Sorrowful, and Glorious Mysteries of the Rosary. I thought 3 was too little and 7 being the next holy number would be more pleasing to God. You might think it is a bit "heavy" praying so much, but it is my peaceful devotion. My first 10 *Hail Marys* include everything I pray for. I think about what I am praying for, bowing down, focusing on His will, and that everything will be okay if I do what God wants. God wants us to do the challenging thing, what is not easy; God wants us to need His help.

I recite *Hail Mary full of grace...*, keeping my mind on the words and meaning them. I imagine things as I am praying, *the Lord is with Thee. Blessed art thou among women,* and I see a queen of heaven, and a tender mother holding the baby Jesus, which puts me in a very good mood. *Holy Mary, Mother of God, pray for us sinners,* and then I prioritize my prayers for others: my immediate family, the kids, family, and the dogs. The second *Hail Marys* I pray for my extended family, friends, people I have met, seen, heard of, or read about. The third (holy number) *Hail Mary*, I pray for the priests, new ones, and the exorcists, the pastors, all holy people, and those trying to help others since those people get attacked by the devil a lot. The fourth *Hail Mary* I pray for people to awaken and for those in purgatory. The fifth *Hail Mary* I pray for aid in crimes against kids such as abuse, torture, and those to be killed, and I pray for their rescuers and cops. The sixth *Hail Mary* I pray for the white hats (heroes), crime, corruption, the cabal and God's justice and mercy. On the seventh *Hail Mary*, I pray for those who are medically challenged with cancer or any other debilitating or fatal condition, mental health, those thinking of abortion and pray for those who help these people. The eighth *Hail Mary* I pray for those in crisis, those contemplating suicide, those who have lost a loved one, those prosecuted for their faith and any other crises, as well as those who can help. The ninth *Hail Mary* I pray for all those who hurt me including -- my parents, Brent and Candy, and Mark. The tenth *Hail Mary* I pray for the Immaculate Heart of Mary and the Sacred Heart of Jesus. I imagine they hurt the most. Throughout all ten *Hail Marys* I also pray for the conversion of sinners because it is what the Virgin Mary asks of us, and the goal is to lead all souls to heaven. It never becomes heavy, it's very alive since I am truly with the Virgin Mary and Jesus.

Just about every morning Michelle prays a rosary along with me while we have breakfast, which is sweet. She is no longer talking or thinking darkly and seems happier. I am sure that praying works. When I only prayed a little, I wasn't getting better. I was undisciplined, getting angry at Bobby, even while knowing anger is a sin. I was only praying three crowns, 12 rosaries, not seven, 28 rosaries. As soon as I began to pray more, everything changed. You must be relentless; when things are difficult, try harder and pray more.

Bobby has always been great about trying harder. He supports my poems on my radio show, "The Cure," as he supports so much that I do. He has ambition for me, as he has for himself, and he acts on his beliefs. It is a tremendous gift for me, and I am greatly blessed by having someone in my life who helps me make my dreams and purpose come true.

People have told me on the show and when they write me that they find my voice soothing and follow me with my prayers and podcast. Now Bobby is encouraging me to give speeches about the spiritual life to help others.

I tried one and I did not think it went well. In fact I thought it was horrible. But then again, Pickpocket (what I call the devil) doesn't like speeches about God so he gets a bit rowdy about stopping you. My daughter, Michelle, who hardly ever compliments me, loved the speech, and was encouraged to be a speaker herself.

But my message in my speech was very clear and maybe that is what is good. Everything bad comes from evil, everything good comes from God. There is no in-between. Everything happens for a reason, and we are the author of our own misery by setting ourselves up for Pickpocket's tricks. We must be vigilant in living a clean, honest and well-meaning life.

God takes care of demons if we pray. I now know the purer a soul you are, the more attacked you will be. We need God on our side. I had to let go of dysfunctional friends who were still acting out. We are called not to be around sin. I am careful whom I let close to me.

And there are always surprises. My sister Michelle had lost her faith; she never smoked, never drank, she was a goody two shoes who never lost her temper. But she got discouraged by our past and for some reason took to the Mormon Church, even though she is a Catholic.

But I prayed for her, sent her a copy of *Freedom through Christ* (by Elza Spaedy, 2020, Tan Books.) and shared the rosary apps I use. Now she is praying rosaries again, her life is on track, and she has her faith in goodness again.

God knows that love must run deep and be willing to go through anything. He even sacrificed his only Son for our souls. That is a deep love.

I finally realized that my priest believes that all of us can be saints and God has a lot in store for us if we give our hearts fully to Him. I also realized that forgiveness never stops; we are going to be constantly called to forgive in relationships -- forgive others and forgive ourselves. Pickpocket is never going to quit trying to trip us up.

I've realized that have to keep asking God for what we need. The prayer reads, *Give us this day our daily bread*, meaning tomorrow we must ask God again for what we need, which has the double benefit of keeping us humble and close to God every day.

I post daily spiritual readings on my social media, all so God can show us so many things. And, believe me, He will.

Chapter 27

Taking the five loaves and the two fish and looking up to heaven, he gave thanks and broke the loaves. Then he gave them to his disciples to distribute to the people. He also divided the two fish among them all.

Mark 6:41

The truth is I am very blessed. I enjoy my life in prayer while I clean; I enjoy the candles in my house, listening to music, and having lots of sunlight in my house. I enjoy my two Maltese and one shih tzu dog (I like the number three) who sleep with me and keep me company. My family is what makes me complete.

No longer vaping or smoking weed since the first day of advent 11-28-2020, no medications for the past seven years, and no therapy is another blessing for me. In other words, I have no need to escape. I put my faith in and get my health from God. Sure, I get down and go through suffering like we all do, but I see suffering as a tool for growth, something that we learn from, even a blessing. I don't mind it. I offer it to God for the sanctification and conversion of souls.

In truth, my vehicles for recovery are prayer, my family, writing and helping others. These ways work for me. For so long, I was unable to say a word about my own life; I was a mixture of pain, guilt, shame, and confusion. Now I can stand up and speak it, face it, write it, and learn from it. Prayer is my source of strength, as well as reading more and more books on the after-effects of what I have been through and spiritual direction.

Miami is a blessing for me, covered in blue skies and surrounded by blue sea everywhere, which is the Virgin Mary's color. That was also the color in my wedding which I dedicated to the Virgin Mary.

There is no longer high drama in my relationships. My relationships are stable since I accepted that other people's behavior does not need to affect mine. I know I can get through anything, with Bobby and with God. Danielle's recovery proved that. Fighting Brent for so many years and winning proved that.

I know I suffered a lot, but it is okay, so did Jesus. Maybe suffering is a privilege because it brings you closer to people and God. All that going to court for 14 years, being treated as less than human, and seeing how much corruption there was in the law (and some lawyers) made me understand Jesus better. But justice did prevail in the end, and so I look at this time as being of the Holy Spirit.

I realize that the truth comes out eventually; it may hurt, it may shock, and it may not be listened to, but it wins out in the end. Those whom you want in your life are the people who can hear the truth and want to transact in the truth. If others refuse to transact in the truth, like Andres and my mother, then let them. Let me celebrate those who can.

Most of us have self-destructive behaviors and nothing worthwhile comes easy, so my path is not unique. We all go through difficulty. I have learned that the path is to love even those who have hurt you, unconditionally (maybe not be around them if they are repetitively cruel) and be there for each other. If you have God in your life, and prayer, and do the right thing, and believe in yourself, you will gain the sense of self to go forward. You might be in tremendous emotional and physical pain as I was, but it is not forever. Solutions will come, change will come, and you can keep growing. We all move towards the light if we are inclined to. If we want that, we will. We just need patience.

It took a long time to think anyone would want to listen to me. Who would want to know someone who did drugs, was an escort and a stripper? Because of that, I often didn't turn to anyone and would suffer whatever I had to in silence. It was Bobby who taught me to turn to someone. Never having had a loving mother, I didn't know you COULD turn to anyone. I now feel sorry for my mother, and it is a tremendous sadness to have no relationship with a mother. It is a big mountain to recover from.

Curiously, we all had to take personality tests at our office, and I was to learn traits about myself that I did not know. I learned I am "an Ace:" decisive, tireless, forthright, goal-oriented and, of course, shielded. I have belief as a strength and of course that has saved me. Harmony is my strongest quality, which is why I think I have survived so much.

It is a shock to me, and probably to anyone who knew me when I was young, that I am the president of our company, and the owner of a medical research company, yes, me, who lived through such instability and at one time could not even hold down a job. But Bobby trusted me completely, even with all our finances. He believed in me. And I rose to the occasion. I feel it is my job to make him happy, keep our staff as a family, be kind, listen to them, create an environment where we all work together joyously. This is my gift, and it is honouring God to answer a sacred call. Mine is to make peace and create a space of trust and fluidity for others. Bobby knew that.

Honestly, I can say I am happy now. I will always suffer from some sadness, but it doesn't last; I know the tools to overcome it. I can help people who have suffered by sharing my own truths and how the sharing can be healing. I can be an activist for good. The fact is, most people in life who see clearly are those who suffered the most. It burns out your fear. You know you can survive. And that is our story to tell.

That is the assurance I can give you, my reader. We can survive and we can love.

It is a fool proof prescription.

Let me share a prayer I really like that helps when one is burdened:

"Heavenly Father, I come before You this moment humbled by Your strength, Your love, Your patience, and Your relentless pursuit of our hearts. Lord, You know my situation better than anyone. Better than even I understand. You also know the weariness that is threatening to consume my existence. The fight within me is dwindling. So, I come to You laying down all my pride. All my striving. All that I hold so firmly in my hand, I come to You and hand it over and ask You to fill it with all that is You. I pray to be strengthened with all Your glorious power so that I will have all the endurance and patience I need. (Col 1:11). I claim Your promise that You will take care of me when I give all these burdens to You. I believe You will not allow me to slip and fall (Ps 55:22) I refuse to be discouraged because You are my God and You will hold me up with Your victorious right hand (Isa 41:10). In the name of Jesus, I pray."

Thank you for reading my story and may God bless you in your journey. As they say, Keep the faith.

About Kharis Publishing

Kharis Publishing, an imprint of Kharis Media LLC, is a leading Christian and inspirational book publisher based in Aurora, Chicago metropolitan area, Illinois. Kharis' dual mission is to give voice to under-represented writers (including women and first-time authors) and equip orphans in developing countries with literacy tools. That is why, for each book sold, the publisher channels some of the proceeds into providing books and computers for orphanages in developing countries so that these kids may learn to read, dream, and grow. For a limited time, Kharis Publishing is accepting unsolicited queries for nonfiction (Christian, self-help, memoirs, business, health and wellness) from qualified leaders, professionals, pastors, and ministers. Learn more at: About Us - Kharis Publishing - Accepting Manuscript

www.ingramcontent.com/pod-product-compliance
Lightning Source LLC
Chambersburg PA
CBHW071755090426
42737CB00012B/1823